1994

1. Ethics

ETHICS FOR DOCTORS, NURSES AND PATIENTS

ETHICS

for

Doctors, Nurses and Patients

H.P. DUNN, M.D.

ALBA·HOUSE NEW·YORK

SOCIETY OF ST. PAUL, 2187 VICTORY BLVD., STATEN ISLAND, NEW YORK 10314

Library of Congress Cataloging-in-Publication Data

Dunn, H.P.
  Ethics for doctors, nurses, and patients / H.P. Dunn.
      p. cm.
   ISBN 0-8189-0688-X
   1. Medical ethics. 2. Catholic Church — Doctrines. 3. Christian
  ethics — Catholic authors.   I. Title.
  R725.56.D86   1994
  174'.2 — dc20   93-44150
                                          CIP

Produced and designed in the United States of America by the
Fathers and Brothers of the Society of St. Paul,
2187 Victory Boulevard, Staten Island, New York 10314,
as part of their communications apostolate.

ISBN: 0-8189-0688-X

Printing Information:

Current Printing - first digit	1	2	3	4	5	6	7	8	9	10

Year of Current Printing - first year shown

1994	1995	1996	1997	1998	1999

DEDICATION

To those uncounted numbers of
admirable doctors, nurses and patients
who day by day aim to live out their
lives in accordance with the basic
virtues of love and justice.

CONTENTS

ETHICS FOR DOCTORS, NURSES AND PATIENTS

CHAPTER 1

AN ETHICAL STATEMENT

The need for medical ethics

At a time when there seems to be an ethical collapse both in society and in the medical profession, there is a parallel upsurge in interest in medical ethics. Twenty years ago, hardly any American medical schools included this subject in the curriculum. Now over half of them have formal courses in ethics. In England there is an Institute of Medical Ethics with its own *Journal*; in 1992 an International Association of Bioethics was launched in Melbourne, Australia; many books are written on the subject; most hospitals now have an Ethics Committee to assess treatments and research projects; and the World Medical Association has issued a series of ethical statements as guides to physicians.

Nevertheless, despite the noble intention of these initiatives the current situation is far from satisfactory. It is sufficient to consider the flourishing euthanasia movement and the global abortion explosion to show that there is a serious confusion of standards. Up to the 1960's these two activities were regarded as the worst examples of unethical conduct; now they are widely accepted, even admired.

Basic assumptions and conventions

I write as a simple practicing obstetrician and gynecologist who, because of the nature of the work, has had to face up to ethical decisions almost daily. I do not pretend to any special philosophical or theological expertise apart from what one learns as an educated layman. My approach will be mainly clinical. It will be based on common sense and the teachings of the Roman Catholic Church.

As my work has been mainly with women, I tend to refer to the patient as "she." If I use the terms "man" or "mankind" it is in the dictionary sense of "a member of the human species." This should not be interpreted as male chauvinism or discrimination against women.

The nature of Medicine

Medicine is a life of service to the patients, to their families, to society. The ideal motto for the physician is: *Caritas et justitia* (Love and justice). Expressed in another way, the purpose of Medicine is: Sometimes to cure; often to relieve; always to console.

CHAPTER 2

A BASIS FOR ETHICS

The nature of law

If one attempts to outline a system of ethics, which is really an expression of some form of law, it is necessary to define who is the lawgiver on which it is based, otherwise the whole concept becomes somewhat arbitrary. This is the weakness of most of the current pronouncements on medical ethics. They derive solely from legislators or from the office bearers of the local medical associations and, while these may be experts in legislation or medical practice, they carry no special weight in the fields of law, philosophy or religion.

Law is of the essence for human beings because it is essential for the proper ordering of society and for guaranteeing the welfare of both the citizens and the state. There are many forms of law, the main ones concerning us here being: divine law, natural moral law, natural physiological law, canon law, civil law, and international law. Of course, there is much overlapping between them all.

It is obvious that the most fundamental and important in this group is divine law, because it depends for its validity on God Himself. It is therefore an impossible anomaly to have a medical ethical statement which is opposed to divine law. Nonetheless, it is not uncommon to find medical authorities and governments making

3

laws or issuing instructions in our day and age which are at variance with that law.

To determine what is the law of God, one must turn to reason and to conscience, which informs us of the instinctive and innate principles of the natural law. These guides are available to everyone, and they have produced such admirable mentors as Hippocrates, Plato and Aristotle. There is also the pre-Christian divine revelation, embodied in the Old Testament. The principles of the Ten Commandments codified the ethical conduct which all previous generations were aware of as the natural law.

Since the time of Christ we must turn to His Church for guidance, because He gave it the authority to teach all nations. The Roman Catholic Church alone claims to be "the one true Church." In the modern world we have not only the "scandal of disunity" but also the scandal of churches holding diametrically opposed views on the medical ethical issues which plague the profession.

Natural moral law

Human beings are ethical creatures. Every day we make scores of ethical decisions, mainly on matters of small practical importance. The basic statement of the natural moral law is: Do good and avoid evil.

But what is "good"? Philosophically speaking the "good" is that which is in conformity with the ultimate truth of a thing, its correspondence with the end for which it was created. In other words, the good is that which is in harmony with the will or law of God.

Equally important is this corollary from the natural law: You may not do evil that good may ensue. The duty to do good is absolute; and equally so is the obligation to avoid evil.

Confusion over this issue is the source of much of the ethical problems faced by doctors, nurses and patients. They perceive that a certain action may be wrong or at the very least distasteful, but conclude that in these serious circumstances it is justified. The end justifies the means.

This, of course, is absolutely wrong. St. Paul was explicit in his condemnation of this approach to moral decision-making in his Letter to the Romans in which he attacked those who accused Christians of holding this position: "And why not say, as some slanderously claim that we *do* say, 'Let's do evil that good may come of it!' Those who say such things are justly condemned!" (Rm 3:8). The end does *not* justify the means.

Anything opposed to the natural law is described as "unnatural." When behavior is described as unnatural, it is because it offends against the natural moral law. Homosexuality and bestiality are examples of unnatural vices, hence immoral. These activities are performed with natural anatomical organs, but they are perversions of the natural physiological design of the reproductive organs.

The mystery of mankind is that we have an innate desire to seek the good; but at the same time a strong inclination to do what is evil, an ineradicable hangover from the Fall. Plato (d. 347 B.C.) stated in *Protagoras*: "To prefer evil to good is inconsistent with human nature." To prefer good to evil is the ideal toward which human nature tends.

Further to confirm that human nature never changes, that the natural law has been recognized from time immemorial, and that great minds have always held that it is never permissible to do evil in the hope of producing a good effect, one need only quote from the *Ethics* of Aristotle (d. 322 B.C.): "There are some actions and emotions whose very names connote baseness, e.g. spite, shamelessness, envy; and among actions adultery, theft and murder. These and similar emotions and actions imply by their very names that they are bad.... It is, therefore, impossible ever to do right in performing them; to perform them is always wrong. In cases of this sort, let us say adultery, rightness and wrongness do not depend on committing it with the right woman at the right time and in the right manner, for the mere fact of committing such action at all is to do wrong."

Some definitions

There is some confusion in this area because of a lack of precision in the terms used.

Ethics is the science of morality.

Morality is the concept of right or wrong conduct. All human actions can be judged as being morally good, bad, or indifferent. Most of our words, deeds, or thoughts are in the last category.

Conscience is the faculty by which we make moral judgments. It is innate, but it can be refined or blunted during our progress through life.

In his public audience on October 15, 1988, Pope John Paul II made some incisive comments which clarified the vexed question of freedom of conscience and how far that concept is valid:

"With the passing of time it is ever more evident how certain attitudes of those claiming the so-called 'right to dissent' have had harmful repercussions on the moral conduct of some of the faithful.

"As I mentioned in my address to the American Bishops in Los Angeles last year: 'It has been noted that there is a tendency on the part of some Catholics to be selective in their adherence to the Church's moral teachings.' Some people appeal to 'freedom of conscience' to justify this way of acting.

"Therefore it is necessary to clarify that it is *not* conscience that establishes what is right and wrong. Using a brilliant expression of (Cardinal) John Henry Newman in his Oxford University sermons (c. 1840), we can say that 'conscience is an instrument for *detecting* moral truth.' Conscience detects moral truth; it interprets a norm, but *it does not create it*."

St. Thomas Aquinas (d. 1274) with his characteristic brilliance addressed himself to this same question.[1] He taught that conscience is the application of knowledge to action. That is, it is a judgment of reason about how we ought to act, based on what we believe to be true. We must always do what we *think* to be good and avoid what we *think* is evil, even if we happen to be mistaken about the facts.

However, he made it clear that an erroneous conscience does

not excuse a person from sin unless he is in error through no fault of his own (invincible ignorance). But if his error is the result of his voluntary neglect of his own moral education, his wrong actions would not excuse him from sin.

Moral assessment

The *morality* of any human action is assessed according to three criteria:

(1) The *action* itself. This may be positive (commission) or negative (omission of a duty). It may involve not only deeds but also thoughts or words. This is the *objective* assessment.
(2) The *intention* in the subject's mind. This is the *subjective* assessment. The truth in this area is difficult to arrive at, and in most cases is known only to the person and to God.
(3) The *circumstances* at the time. As the legal saying goes, "Circumstances alter cases"; and, when it comes to making a judgment, "Hard cases make bad law."

For persons with a refined conscience, number (1) is the most important factor. If an action is wrong, it may not be done, even if the refusal to do it involves some risk. But in the modern world it is common to see numbers (2) and (3) elevated to the position of primary importance. This is known as "situation ethics" of which the foremost exponent is Joseph Fletcher, Ph.D., lately of the Harvard Divinity School, Boston.

Papal authority

Persons of good will find that they agree with most of the principles outlined here.[2] On a few issues we will agree to disagree. The Pope has the right and the duty to pronounce on moral problems and he deserves respect and obedience, not only by virtue of his office but also because of the assurance given by Christ to Peter that He would be with him (and his successors) "all days, even to the end of the world" (Matthew 28:20).

The Church did not devise these moral judgments on her own initiative. She merely elucidates the principles given by God in the Decalogue thousands of years before the Church was founded, and she applies them to specific cases. Proof of this assertion lies in the fact that, if we were practicing Medicine before the Christian era, as Hippocrates was, we would adhere to exactly the same principles as are outlined here.

Are moral principles absolute or relative?

When this fundamental question arises, society in general opts for relativism because it makes life easier and it justifies practically everything. Persons of deep religious faith, though, are not hesitant to declare that the only logical option is for the absolute. The idea of a God who never changes, who is the same "yesterday, today and forever" (Hebrews 13:8), and whose teaching never varies is common not only to the religions of the East but to those of the West as well. Some actions are always wrong, just as some (for example, love and justice) are always right. We have an absolute duty to do good and avoid evil in serious matters of conscience. Our duty to love and adore God is unchangeable and inescapable. At the other extreme there is an absolute prohibition on blasphemy, that is, the calculated and malicious insult to God, not the casual, vulgar and thoughtless profanity of uncouth conversation. Another example is adultery, which being a treachery and an infidelity is always wrong.

The existence of law logically implies rights and duties, rewards for obedience and penalties for infringement. A shallow statement which is frequently heard is: "The state cannot legislate morality." Of course the civil law cannot force moral living on its citizens — even the Church can only persuade them to adopt the common virtues — but the fact is that the right ordering of society is possible only when individual citizens are living virtuous lives. Their several interests happen to coincide. The dictum quoted above is often used in an attempt to persuade the state to adopt a neutral stance and not to impede a social movement, for example, the legalization of prostitution.

To quote St. Augustine: "Morality is obedience to law." Obviously this applies to both moral law and civil law, with the proviso that an unjust civil law does not bind.

Another similar catchword is the "victimless" crime. This concept implies that private evil actions, such as addiction to pornography or drugs, harm no one but the addict, therefore they should be removed from the supervision of the state. It should be obvious to everyone that this view is erroneous. Since we are social beings, members of the great human family, if one of us is afflicted we all suffer. And the evil that takes place behind closed doors soon spills out to affect the larger community. The taxpayer ultimately foots the bill for many "private" vices.

Sin

This is a subject that no one likes to discuss, but in a treatise on ethics it is impossible to avoid. Sin is an offence against the moral code, and it can be classified as either serious (mortal) or minor (venial). These terms are unfashionable but they are nonetheless real. Mortal sin kills the life of grace in the soul. St. John uses this term when he tells us that "there is a sin which is mortal... All wrongdoing is sinful, but there are some sins which are not mortal" (1 Jn 5:16-17).

The traditional list of *The Seven Deadly Sins* is an inspired concept which accurately describes the frail human condition. They are set out in descending order of seriousness — if one can postulate a gradation in deadliness. Comments are made on their importance for medical practitioners.

(1) *Pride*. First in gravity, first in importance, first in history. Lucifer was guilty of the sin of pride when he uttered his epic *"Non serviam!"* ("I will not serve God") and the Archangel Michael thrust him out of Heaven forever (Revelation 12:7). In reference to this historic event Christ said: "I saw Satan cast down from Heaven like a bolt of lightning" (Luke 10:18).

It is salutary to recall that, as St. Peter said, Satan even now "goes about like a roaring lion, seeking someone to devour" (1 Peter 5:8). C.S. Lewis points out in *The Screwtape Letters* that the Devil's favorite ploy is to persuade people that he does not exist, and in this deception he is remarkably successful. He is to this day the sinister figure behind all human evil: wars, torture, cruelty, injustice, and every other frightening sin which human beings commit.

The first sin in *human* history was also one of pride, when the Serpent (the Devil) persuaded Eve to eat "the fruit of the tree of the knowledge of good and evil" (Genesis 2:17). He appealed to her pride — "If you have the knowledge of good and evil you will be like gods!" What a monumental mistake! Knowledge of evil, which in biblical language means the personal experience of evil, brings only sadness, suffering and death.

Pride might very well be *the* predominant fault of all professionals, physicians, health-care givers and clergy not excluded. If we would occasionally remind ourselves that we have hardly increased life expectancy from the biblical seventy, "or eighty for those who are strong" (Ps 90:10), then perhaps we would be a little more humble.

(2) *Avarice*. Another genius, Dante Alighieri (d. 1321), pointed out the significance of this vice in the first Canto of his *Divine Comedy*. In it he describes how he entered Hell (the Inferno) through a gateway with the words emblazoned above it: "Abandon hope all you who enter here" (*Lasciata ogni speranza voi ch'entrate*). Almost immediately he encountered a lion, a leopard and a she-wolf. These represented the predominant sins of the three age groups: the young, lust; the old, avarice; and the middle-aged, pride.

It is a common observation that as persons age they tend to become avaricious and miserly. Physicians are often accused of being covetous and enamored of money. It is not money itself which is evil, but an undue attachment to it: "The *love of money* is the root of all evil" (2 Timothy 6:10). It is quite right and proper for physicians and other health-care workers to earn a good income in order to care for their families, to enable their children to achieve an education equal to their own, to keep up-to-date in their profession, to be well-equipped and to travel to conferences. Very few become obsessed with money; and most of them, truth be told, provide free treatment to a growing number of indigent patients.

(3) *Lust.* For the average person, this is a common sin. Few have the opportunity or reason to murder, or to embezzle a million dollars, or to deal in drugs — but sex is there all day and every day, ready to express love in marriage or to wreak havoc in persons' lives when misused outside this normal state.

Patients have a right to expect their health-care givers to control their sexual inclinations. Promiscuous physicians are a menace. Hippocrates saw clearly the risks that the doctor's privileged position presents for both patient and physician. In his day and age homo- and heterosexual vices were as common as they are today, and slaves were often the victims of the sexual approaches of their masters. Therefore in his *Oath* he stated: "Into whatever houses I enter I will go into them for the benefit of the sick and will abstain from every voluntary act of mischief or corruption, and further from the seduction of males or females, bond or free." Since it would be impossible to adhere to these high principles without a vibrant spiritual life, we can deduce that he must have been a man of prayer in his polytheistic world.

(4) *Anger.* There is such a thing as righteous anger, as Christ demonstrated when He drove the moneylenders out of the Temple (Mark 15:17). Still we are advised to be "slow to anger" (Nehemiah 9:17). Our aim should be never to become angry with our patients,

however stupid, inconsiderate or irritating they might be. There is only endless patience. How often has an importunate patient turned out to have had some serious pathology, or their unreasonable behavior attributable to a slow-growing cerebral tumor.

(5) *Envy*. None of us easily admits to being envious. But what if one of our more "undeserving" colleagues is unexpectedly awarded a travelling scholarship? "How could the trustees have overlooked our much more valuable contribution?" Beware the green-eyed monster! Congratulate your colleague on his or her success. Do we find ourselves secretly pleased when a top surgeon gets into all sorts of trouble and has a disastrous experience in the operating room? It's so easy to become mean-spirited.

(6) *Gluttony*. Sometimes at medical dinners we eat and drink too much. And that too often leads to the modern sin of "drinking and driving." This sin of gluttony (which always seems to apply to others, not to us!) also embraces such faults as drug addiction and other forms of excessive self-indulgence. It is impossible to live a virtuous life without some penitential discipline in our lives. Fasting on a regular basis (once a week, for example) is a good way to curb our wayward appetites.

(7) *Sloth*. This seems a harmless sort of fault, but it almost always leads to serious problems. For most of us, it might take the form of dragging our feet at the clinic, or neglecting poor patients, or being reluctant to get up at night to help junior residents when they need our support. But the most serious variety of this sin is moral sloth — being too lazy or indifferent to fulfill our religious duties of prayer and church attendance; or to inform ourselves about the important spiritual and moral issues of the day.

Culpability

In traditional moral teaching, for a sin to be committed three elements must be present:

(a) *Grave matter* — There is usually not much dispute about this, but some people are so scrupulous that they see evil in everything they do. Scrupulosity beyond a certain point becomes a psychiatric problem.

(b) *Full knowledge* — Obviously a clear appreciation of objective evil is often lacking. For the average person who does not have proper clerical guidance, some activities (for example, contraception) are not perceived as wrong in essence. In such cases culpability may be nil.

(c) *Full consent of the will* — If this is absent, there is no culpability. This probably applies often to those who fight temptation as hard as they can and still find themselves failing to be wholly victorious over it. Sexual offences in the young may be a case in point.

The moral principle of the double effect

Every human action has multiple repercussions, dozens of effects, and this complicates its moral assessment. But there are usually two principal effects on which we can concentrate. We can assume that the main effect is morally good and desirable, but should one pursue it if the secondary effect is evil and undesirable?

A gynecologist eschews sterilizing operations, but whenever he performs a hysterectomy for some indisputable indication, he indirectly sterilizes the patient. Is this permissible? Of course.

If a cancer of the cervix is discovered during early pregnancy, the standard treatment (which may include the use of deep X-rays or the insertion of radium or cesium) may licitly be directed at the malignancy. Any ill-effects on the fetus are tolerated as indirect and inescapable, foreseen but not directly desired. The fetus will probably succumb and go on to spontaneous miscarriage, but at least one case has been reported in which the baby survived and was born with a bald patch on its head caused by the proximity of the radium.

Regrettably, the usual management is first to abort the fetus and with that out of the way, aggressive treatment of the tumor is instituted. Direct abortion is wrong in all circumstances. In fact, it is doubtful if this management produces significantly better results in the long run. The prognosis for the mother is already poor and these procedures may end up with a dead mother as well as a dead baby.

Occasionally we have a brave mother who decides for religious and philosophical reasons that she will refuse any treatment until the baby is mature enough to be delivered, usually by Caesarean section. This means delaying her own treatment for a few months (never more than six months; sometimes as little as three). Such a delay in this type of tumor probably does not make much difference in the ultimate prognosis, but it at least ensures that the baby will live. What could be more Christ-like? "Greater love than this no man has, than that he lay down his life for his friend" (John 15:13). (For "man" read "woman"; for "friend" read "child.") This heroic courage is not unknown in modern times.[3]

Moralists sum up the principle of the double effect in the following way:

1. The act itself must be morally good, or at least indifferent.
2. The good effect of the act must precede the evil effect, or at least be simultaneous with it.
3. The motive behind the act must be to achieve the good effect, never the evil effect, even though this is foreseen and permitted.
4. The good effect must be sufficiently desirable to outweigh the evil effect.

While this analysis may seem ponderous, in the clinical situation, the correct judgment can be arrived at almost instantly.

Choosing the lesser of two evils

This common ethical dilemma is sometimes confused with the principle of the double effect, possibly because they both involve the number "two" — two effects; two evils. The dictum, choosing the lesser of two evils, is often quoted to justify actions which are morally wrong — and that is never permissible.

Example No. 1: Planned Parenthood in their zeal to have every teenager equipped with contraceptives consider that this is an either/or situation, and they choose contraception as a lesser evil than abortion or AIDS. (In actual fact, they often end up with both evils, but that is another matter.) Each of these alternatives is wrong in essence and therefore cannot be countenanced.

Example No. 2: You are driving down a steep street when your hydraulic brake fluid hose ruptures. Your brakes fail. Ahead is a line of school children crossing the road, followed by several older women. You have time only to turn towards the women, instinctively deciding that hitting them rather than the children is the lesser of two evils.

The fallacy behind the common misinterpretation represented by Example No. 1 is that it fails to distinguish between evil actions which the subject directly sets in motion, and those (Example No. 2) which have not been initiated by the individual. In the first case, the person is completely responsible. In the second, he is caught up in a tide of wrong-doing but he tries to minimize the potential for harm.

Therefore: we may sometimes *permit* the lesser of two evils; but we may *never willingly commit* any evil, whether lesser or greater.

Principles of cooperation

Many physicians agonize over situations in which they seem to be obliged to assist in actions which they know to be wrong. Is it possible to work out a *modus vivendi* with evil, if only for the sake of peace? Some of these dilemmas seem incapable of resolution, but it is useful to analyze the various degrees of cooperation in what is objectively wrongdoing.

The differing degrees of cooperation can be conveniently described as: direct or indirect; proximate or remote; formal (giving advice or encouragement) or material (providing the means required in the evil venture).

Direct cooperation is always wrong. It is the equivalent in legal terms to being an accessory before or after the fact. Indirect or remote forms may bear little moral guilt.

As an example of the application of these principles in a clinical situation, let us consider the distasteful subject of abortion because it is such a clear-cut issue, and assess its ethical impact on all those involved. The basic assumption is that induced abortion (that is, the direct killing of the child, of whatever maturity, in the womb) is serious wrongdoing, often a crime, always a sin. As always, if the subject suffers from ignorance or duress, there may be diminished culpability.

(1) *The surgeon (gynecologist)* — he is intimately involved. His cooperation is direct, proximate and material, therefore this is a serious moral fault. He usually makes the excuses that: "the end justifies the means"; the law allows it; if he refuses the patient may go to an illegal abortionist whose operative technique will be inferior to his; or she might commit suicide; or the child will be labelled "unwanted"; or his refusal might harm his professional career.

(2) *The patient* — her cooperation is identical with that of the surgeon. Nevertheless, it is almost certain that in the majority of cases there is so much fear, distress, ignorance and duress from family members and others that her guilt may be minimal.

(3) *The anesthesiologist* — his contribution to the operation is so essential that his degree of cooperation is only slightly less than that of the surgeon. Some moralists claim that, if he is a full-time hospital employee, he may accept every case on the operating list without demur. However, now that his speciality is well established in its own right, it is

difficult to accept that excuse. He would also be worried that his advancement in his career may be impeded if he refused to cooperate.

A useful escape for the sincere but confused person is the theory of *Probabilism*. This means that, if he can find a reputable moral theologian who approves his stance on cooperation (or whatever) he is entitled to act in this way with a clear conscience.

(4) *The surgical assistant (if any)* — his cooperation is also direct, proximate and material. He, too, should decline to assist in this work unless he gets caught in an emergency situation and cannot withdraw from the operation without increasing the risk to the patient.

(5) *The scrub-up nurse* — she is also intimately involved in the procedure and must accept responsibility for her cooperation.

(6) *The unscrubbed (or circulating) nurse* — she does not directly act in the abortion but her indirect and material cooperation is not insignificant. Her situation is not crystal clear, and she could take refuge in a probable opinion without becoming too scrupulous.

(7) *The ward doctor (resident)* — who simply sees the patient after admission and checks her fitness for operation. His cooperation is indirect and remote, and therefore it is probably licit. But he should not give the impression to the patient that he approves of the procedure. His best plan is to say nothing; but if the patient asks his advice about the matter, that gives him the justification to express his opinion.

(8) *The ward nurse* — who prepares the patient for operation and gives the pre-medication. Her situation is almost identical with that of the ward doctor.

(9) *The general picture* — It is easy to imagine the pressures, sometimes explicit coercion, that junior medical and nursing staff experience in these matters. Such unfair

manipulation should be foreign to these so-called "liberal" professions. The fact that medical and nursing authorities have failed to protect their junior members in this matter is an injustice that ought to be remedied.

The dilemmas referred to above assume that the abortions are incidental operations in a general hospital. If they are taking place in a ward or a free-standing clinic which is devoted solely to this procedure, the whole ethical picture changes radically. In those circumstances everyone on the staff, with the exception of cooks, cleaners and maintenance personnel, shares in the injustice being perpetrated and nothing can excuse their cooperation.

Abortion facilitators — these people are not doctors or nurses but, for the sake of completeness, their position in this global tragedy should be commented on. They are the politicians who legalize abortion; the opinion-formers in society (writers, journalists, lecturers, church leaders); abortion-promoting organizations; counsellors; manufacturers of equipment or drugs used in these procedures, their staffs and shareholders.

All these are guilty of cooperation which is indirect, remote, formal and sometimes material. Some of them may be able to claim ignorance as an excuse — the views of some are naive in the extreme — but the majority who live by abortion must accept full responsibility.

Veritatis Splendor (1993)

In this brilliantly intellectual encyclical Pope John Paul II shows clearly that there is an absolute standard of ethics. These principles are unchanging from age to age and they apply to all people of all races and all cultures. He shows how the modern concepts of proportionalism, consequentialism, pragmatism, the fundamental option, etc. are false and inadequate guides. The natural moral law is imprinted in every human heart, a direct gift from God.

CHAPTER 3

THE OFFICIAL ETHICAL CODES

Hippocrates

The most famous of the medical ethical guides is the *Hippocratic Oath*. Hippocrates (460-377 B.C.) lived on the island of Cos, and such was the force of his intelligence and his natural virtue that his code of conduct has guided physicians right up to the 20th century — but now for the first time the profession has largely abandoned many of his principles. The ethical problems confronting the physician in the 4th century B.C. were much the same in essence as they are now, but in the modern world the ethical dilemmas are more common and more complex.

Few medical schools administer the original Oath to their graduating students. Many (out of fear or embarrassment?) opt for a watered down version. "Fearlessness is the first requisite of spirituality," to quote Mahatma Gandhi. "Cowards can never be moral." Medical students really should insist that their professors arrange a public recital of the Hippocratic Oath.

The Hippocratic Oath

"I swear by Apollo, the physician, and Aesculapius and Hygeia and All-heal, and all the gods and goddesses that, according to my ability and judgment, I will keep this Oath and stipulation —

"To reckon him who taught me this Art equally dear to me as my parents, to share my substance with him and relieve his necessities if required; to look upon his offspring on the same footing as my own brothers, and to teach them this Art if they shall wish to learn it, without fee or stipulation.

"By precept, lecture and every other mode of instruction I will impart a knowledge of the Art, to my own sons and those of my teachers and to disciples bound by a stipulation and oath according to the law of medicine, but to none others.

"I will follow that system of regimen which, according to my ability, I consider for the benefit of my patients and abstain from whatever is deleterious and mischievous. I will give no deadly medicine to anyone if asked, nor suggest such counsel; and in like manner I will not give to a woman a pessary to produce abortion.

"With purity and holiness I will pass my life and practice my Art. I will not cut a person who is suffering with a stone but will leave this to be done by men who are practitioners of this work.

"Into whatever houses I enter I will go into them for the benefit of the sick and will abstain from every voluntary act of mischief and corruption; and further from the seduction of females or males, freemen or slaves.

"Whatever in connection with my professional practice, or not in connection with it, I may see or hear in the lives of men which ought not be spoken of abroad, I will not divulge, as reckoning that all such should be kept secret.

"While I continue to keep this oath unviolated may it be granted to me to enjoy life and the practice of the Art, respected by all men at all times, but, should I trespass and violate this oath, may the reverse be my lot."

The Declaration of Professional Dedication

As an example of ethical emasculation, take the following *Declaration of Professional Dedication* which the graduating class in a nearby Medical School make:

"I solemnly promise to practice the art of Medicine with due care and conduct becoming a physician. In the exercise of my profession I will ever have in mind the care of the sick and the well-being of the healthy. In the furtherance of these ends I will use all my knowledge and will strive to perfect my judgment. I will furthermore keep silence on any matters I may witness or hear in the course of my professional work which it would be improper for me to divulge.

"I promise, as a graduate in medicine, that I will promote the welfare and maintain the reputation of the medical profession. I will also accept my responsibility to pass on the knowledge I have gained and recognize my debt to my preceptors."

Note that there is no mention of euthanasia, abortion, purity, holiness, or the seduction of patients. How could anyone prefer this pap to Hippocrates?

The Code of Maimonides

Maimonides, the great Jewish scholar, philosopher and physician (1135-1204), was born in Spain and died in Egypt. His famous Code is the only one to compare with that of Hippocrates. The former's philosophy was monotheistic, the latter's polytheistic.

"O God, Thou hast formed the body of man with infinite goodness. Thou hast united in him innumerable forces incessantly at work like so many instruments, so as to preserve in its entirety this beautiful house containing his immortal soul and those forces act with all the order, concord and harmony imaginable. But if weakness or violent passion disturb this harmony, these forces act against one another and the body returns to the dust from whence it came.

"Thou sendest then to man Thy Messengers, the diseases which announce the approach of danger, and bid him prepare to overcome them. The Eternal Providence has appointed me to watch over the life and health of Thy creatures. May the love of my art actuate me at all times. May neither avarice, nor miserliness, nor the thirst for glory or for a great reputation engage my mind; for, enemies of truth and philanthropy, they could easily deceive me and make me forgetful of my lofty aim of doing good for Thy children.

"Endow me with strength of heart and mind, so that both may be ready to serve the rich and the poor, the good and the wicked, friend and enemy, and that I may never see the patient as anything else but a fellow-creature in pain.

"If physicians more learned than I wish to counsel me, inspire me with confidence in and obedience towards the recognition of them, for the study of science is great. It is not given to one alone to see all that others see.

"May I be moderate in everything except in the knowledge of this science; so far as it is concerned, may I be insatiable; grant me the strength and opportunity always to correct what I have acquired, always to extend its domain; for knowledge is boundless and the spirit of man can also extend indefinitely, daily to enrich itself with new acquirements. Today he can discover his errors of yesterday, and tomorrow he may obtain new light on what he thinks himself sure of today.

"O God, Thou hast appointed me to watch over the life and death of Thy creatures. Here I am, ready for my vocation. Amen."

This is as much a prayer as an ethical statement. There is praise of God for the wonders of His Creation; our duty to the sick; love of medicine, of scientific knowledge; avoidance of avarice and of pride; respect for older physicians. The virtues of purity and holiness are implied. But there is no specific mention of professional secrets, abortion, euthanasia, or the seduction of patients.

The Declaration of Geneva

This document was adopted by the World Medical Association in 1948 as "the modern version of the Hippocratic Oath." The text, with my comments in brackets, reads as follows:

"At the time of being admitted as a member of the medical profession I solemnly pledge myself to consecrate my life to the service of humanity. I will give to my teachers the respect and gratitude which is their due. I will practice my profession with conscience and dignity. [Too vague.] I will respect the secrets which are confided to me, even after the patient has died. I will maintain by all means in my power the honor and the noble traditions of the medical profession. My colleagues will be my brothers. I will not permit considerations of religion, nationality, race, party politics or social standing to intervene between my duty and my patient. [This seems to imply that a religious doctor will not treat all patients fairly, but an irreligious one will do so. The reverse is probably the case.]

"I will maintain the utmost respect for human life from the time of conception. [This appears to rule out abortion.] Even under threat I will not use my medical knowledge contrary to the laws of humanity. [This refers to the natural moral law; and our repudiation of inhumane acts.] I make these promises solemnly, freely and upon my honor."

Note the differences from the Hippocratic Oath: no specific rejection of euthanasia; no mention of the seduction of patients; and no reference to a personal life of holiness and purity.

The International Code of Medical Ethics

This document, formulated by the World Medical Association in 1949, says (in summary):

Duties of doctors — to maintain the highest professional conduct towards individuals and society [too vague]; not to be influenced by money; avoid self-advertisement; preserve professional independence; avoid dichotomy [fee-splitting]; not to weaken human resistance except in the course of proper medical treatment [that is, not to serve the state through torture or psychiatric manipulation]; to be careful in publishing new or unorthodox treatments; care in writing certificates; "preserve human life from conception until death" [this excluded abortion and euthanasia, but was soon to become a dead letter]; loyalty to the patient; duty to provide consultation; confidentiality; providing emergency treatment.

The Declaration of Helsinki

First published in 1964, it was revised in Tokyo in 1975. It is an admirable statement of the principles governing medical research. All research carries some element of risk as well as benefit to the patients.

The worst chapter in the history of Medicine was written in Nazi Germany where doctors used concentration camp prisoners and psychiatric patients for experimental purposes. Many of their schemes were diabolical. An interesting reflection is that probably not a single useful medical advance came from all this pseudo-scientific manipulation of human beings. One reason is that the genuine researcher must have an inflexible attachment to the truth, because all science is based on true observations. Truth is one aspect of justice. Anyone who is unjust must necessarily abandon his devotion to the truth. Science has, therefore, an inescapable moral quality.

The main points in this *Declaration* were:

— only properly qualified physicians should be permitted to undertake research;
— independent ethical committees were to check on protocols and give permission for experiments;
— the possible benefits to the subject must be greater than the risks;

— "the interest of the subject must always prevail over those of society and of science";
— respect for the privacy and dignity of the subject;
— genuine and freely given informed consent.

The Declaration of Sydney

The advent of organ transplantation made this *Declaration*, published in 1968, necessary as a guide to determining the time of death of the comatose donor. "Brain death" has displaced "cardiac death" as the essential criterion; and the diagnosis must be made before there is organ death. It is obvious that the clinical assessment must always be imprecise and therefore arbitrary; but on the other hand there is no call for excessive scrupulosity. In practice, it becomes mainly a diagnosis that the dying process is irreversible and therefore the life support systems may be disconnected.

The most important sentence in the *Declaration* reads: "If transplantation of an organ is involved, the decision that death exists should be made by one or more physicians; and the physicians determining the moment of death should in no way be immediately concerned with the performance of the transplant." This makes for objectivity. But it is incorrect to say that "death exists" or refer to "the moment of death." The patient is not dead until *after* life support has been withdrawn.

The Declaration of Oslo

This *Statement on Therapeutic Abortion*, published in 1970, was made necessary by the worldwide wave of permissive abortion legislation and the enthusiasm with which doctors welcomed it, performing vast numbers of induced abortions. A good global estimate is about 50 million cases every year. Such a public repudiation of the Hippocratic Oath created an embarrassing dilemma for the medical authorities.

157, 168

The feeble nature of this *Declaration* suggests that it might have been better to have said nothing at all and to have accepted mutely that doctors, as much as their patients, have become besotted with the sexual revolution, of which abortion is one essential facet.

It starts off by recalling the *Declaration of Geneva*: "I will maintain the utmost respect for human life from the time of conception." This is, of course, contradictory, even absurd, if abortion is at the same time permitted. Its most important clause states: "Abortion should be performed only as a therapeutic measure." This is wishful thinking, since about 97 percent of modern abortions are performed for social or economic reasons. "Therapeutic" is a bland and misleading adjective because there is no disease for which abortion is a therapy. There are now *no* medical indications to justify abortion.

The Declaration of Tokyo

There is a nobility about this statement (published in 1975) which was necessitated by the increase of cruel dictatorships that seek to involve the medical profession in their unjust tyrannies.

"The doctor shall not countenance, condone or participate in the practice of torture or other forms of cruel, inhuman or degrading procedures, whatever the offence of which the victim... is suspected, accused or found guilty, and whatever the victim's beliefs or motives, and in all situations, including armed conflict and civil strife." In addition, a doctor will not be present during torture or interfere in a hunger strike.

The Declaration of Lisbon

Various inalienable rights of the patient were reaffirmed in this 1981 statement: to be able to choose one's own doctor; to accept or refuse treatment; to confidentiality; to have access to one's minister of religion; to die with dignity.

Other Declarations

One encouraging sequel to these *Declarations* has been the formation in Britain of the Helsinki Medical Group, who are concerned at the way one of the Helsinki statements was being trampled on, vis.: "The research on man, the interests of science and society should never take precedence over the considerations related to the well-being of the subject."

In a letter to *The Times* (February 13, 1985), Sir John Peel and twenty other Fellows of the Royal College of Obstetricians and Gynaecologists who formed the Group deplored the recommendations of Dame Mary Warnock's Committee (on *in vitro* fertilization). The Committee's views on embryo research, they said, "reduce the status of the human embryo to that of an experimental animal, contravene the code of medical ethics, and must be rejected." Admirable and remarkable!

Another *Declaration* on euthanasia was made in Madrid in 1987; and also a further *Declaration* on organ transplantation. In Vienna in 1988 there was an unusual *Declaration* on environmental and demographic issues. It deplored the degradation of the environment, the loss of top soil and of oil reserves, and the "exponential" growth of population. What, one wonders, do these doctors know about oil or soil? And can they be unaware that the real risk in the West is *de*population not *over*population? The punch-line came in the recommendations: universal family planning. It was obviously promoted by Planned Parenthood.

The *Helsinki Declaration* was updated in Hong Kong in 1989. And in 1990 a *Declaration* outlawing chemical and biological weapons was agreed upon in Rancho Mirage, California.

Similar resolutions with medical repercussions (especially in the field of euthanasia) have come from the United Nations. The most important ones are: *Declaration on the Rights of the Child* (1959); *On the Rights of Mentally Retarded Persons* (1971); and *On the Rights of Disabled Persons* (1975).

An Islamic Code

In 1985, the International Organisation of Islamic Medicine published the following *Code of Medical Ethics* which was formulated by an Egyptian gynecologist, Professor Hassan Hathout, of the University of Kuwait:

"I swear by God the Almighty —

to regard God in carrying out my profession;

to protect human life in all stages and under all circumstances, doing my utmost to rescue it from death, malady, pain and anxiety; to keep people's dignity, cover their privacies and lock up their secrets;

to be all the way an instrument of God's mercy, extending my medical care to near and far, virtuous and sinner, friend and enemy;

to strive in the pursuit of knowledge and harnessing it for the benefit but not the harm of mankind;

to revere my teachers, teach my juniors, and be brother to members of the medical profession, joined in piety and charity; to live my faith in private and public, avoiding whatever blemishes me in the eyes of God, His Apostle and my fellow faithful; and may God be witness to this Oath."

This is a touching revelation of personal holiness and nobility of character. There is no specific reference to the matters mentioned previously, namely, abortion, euthanasia, seduction of patients, or participating in cruel and inhuman punishments. But they are excluded by implication.

A Christian Code of Medical Ethics

The personal codes listed above are from pagan (Hippocrates), Jewish and Muslim sources. The question arises: why is there not a similar Christian pledge? The Church has made innumerable official statements on the complex ethical problems confronting the doctor in the modern world, therefore there seems to be no need for any additional guide but, on the other hand, a brief professional statement would have some esthetic and historical value. To provide a parallel with the previous Oaths it should be written more appropriately by a physician than by a Church authority. The following is offered to make good that deficiency.

"O God, in the name of the Father, the Son and the Holy Spirit, I pledge that in the practice of Medicine I shall with Your help adhere to the principles of love and justice. I shall make the service and welfare of my patient my first duty, which will take precedence over the interests of society or the state.

"Anything which the patient tells me in confidence will be respected and will not be revealed during life or after death.

"I shall not participate in or facilitate artificial contraception, sterilization or induced abortion. I shall not directly bring about the death of any patient, normal or abnormal, healthy or in a terminal illness.

"I shall accept with gratitude any financial rewards which You grant me but shall not allow the pursuit of wealth to dominate my practice or to influence my clinical decisions.

"I shall regard my teachers with gratitude and respect, and I shall foster among my colleagues an atmosphere of friendship and cooperation. In presenting scientific papers I shall repudiate any dishonesty, knowing that we have a duty to truth in our elucidation of the mysteries of Your creation in the human body.

"In purity and holiness I shall pass my life and practice my profession. My soul will be strengthened by daily prayer, weekly Mass and frequent reception of Your sacraments.

"I ask the Blessed Virgin Mary and St. Joseph to bless my family life, and I pray that You will give me a share in the wisdom and courage of Our Lord Jesus Christ in undertaking this medical apostolate. Amen."

CHAPTER 4

RELATIONSHIP OF DOCTOR TO PATIENT

The roles of doctor and patient

In the interests of justice, efficiency and a harmonious relationship, it is important for both doctor and patient to appreciate their individual roles. The doctor is the servant of the patient — but not the patient's slave. The idea seems to be current, especially in obstetrics, that the patient may "order" the doctor to do anything she wishes. The truth is that he aims to serve her best interests, even if his decisions are not perceived by her in that light.

"I want / don't want labor induced." "I want a Caesarean." "I don't want a forceps delivery." "I want an abortion." "I don't want an episiotomy." These demands stem from the popular view that the amateur is as good as the professional in making these decisions, which is plainly untrue. She cannot possibly understand the implications of the demands listed. When she employs a physician he becomes her "medical adviser" and there should be no misconception as to who is advising whom. If the patient is dissatisfied, the doctor can withdraw from the case and she can transfer to another.

The doctor does not have authority over the patient — there is no such thing as "doctor's orders," only advice. If the patient is unhappy with that, one or the other party should seek a second opinion. This is a great protection which is only rarely offered in other professions.

May doctors or nurses strike?

In many countries there are reports of doctors and nurses going on strike, something that was never heard of in the past. The issue is commonly about pay or working conditions. Once young men and women have contracted to assist in the care of patients as members of the medical profession, they may never strike, however unsatisfactory their working conditions might be. They have an implicit duty not to abandon those who have entrusted themselves to their care, and justice demands that this may never be renounced. The rights of the patients supersede those of the medical and nursing staff. The latter may resign and seek employment elsewhere, but they should never bring the work of the hospital to a halt, endangering the life and well-being of their patients.

This onerous duty should be perceived as reasonable. Society has long recognized this obligation on the part of many other classes of essential workers — mothers (!), clergy, firemen, police, soldiers, sailors, teachers, suppliers of food, water and shelter, and many others.

Duty to patients

We have a duty to care equally for all patients, however trying, obnoxious, unrewarding or repulsive they may be. We must give ordinary care to the unborn child whom we cannot see, the senile, the terminally ill, the anencephalic baby who has no prospect of living. They are all human beings, our brothers and sisters, children of God.

Informed consent

Patients have the right to know the nature of their illness and what lines of treatment are available; then they can give their appropriate consent. If the treatment is untried or experimental, they should know all about the benefits and risks involved. In most cases, patients leave these decisions to their physicians.

But in recent years, the situation has swung so far in favor of "information" that it has verged on the absurd. Common sense is needed. It is often impossible to convey to the lay person the complexity of some therapeutic decision-making. In obstetrics it has become a nightmare. Labor is like a battle, the situation changing from hour to hour and during the expulsion stage from minute to minute. If there is any abnormality before delivery, the obstetrician has several differential diagnoses running through his mind but he knows when to say nothing. At a time like this, when the risk to the baby is at a maximum (but most people are unaware of this), it is impossible to discuss with the patient every possible complication or drug effect.

Many physicians have given up the unequal struggle, opted for "defensive medicine" (the doctor defending himself against the patients), and put the decisions onto the woman or her husband. "You tell me what you want me to do, a Caesarean or a forceps delivery." This is an abrogation of duty and responsibility.

Informed consent is an ideal — but it is often an impossible ideal. In the profession there is widespread disenchantment with the concept, as the following quotes from the literature will show.

In an editorial, Dr. R.R. Faden stated: ". . . the proposal [to enforce informed consent] may reinforce the already prevalent view that informed consent is a bureaucratic legal nonsense."[1]

A similar opinion was expressed in another editorial by Dr. W.D. Woods: "Thus, to speak of informed consent in regard to complicated medical procedures that are not easily understood by a layman is a contradiction in terms . . . Indeed the phrase is so overused that it has lost all legally significant meaning."[2]

Further, Dr. W.A. Silverman chose a striking title for his article and wrote: "It has been impossible to devise informed consent practices that satisfy in full competing moral imperatives of respect for autonomy, concern for beneficence [towards the patient] with emphasis on the value of health and a vigil for justice."[3]

Problem Case No. 1

My patient was a lovely looking young woman having her first baby. When she was about six months pregnant, her husband had to go overseas on a business trip. While away he had too much to drink and went with a prostitute. After his return, not knowing that he had contracted a venereal disease (now called a "sexually transmitted disease" — STD, but it means the same thing), he had intercourse with his wife.

He came to me shamefacedly and worried that he might have infected his wife. Would I need to tell her? Making a specious excuse, but without actually telling a falsehood, I took a vaginal swab and sure enough there was the evidence of gonorrhea. Fortunately it was before the days of aggressive questioning of everything we do. I made another excuse of "a slight infection" and gave her a single injection of a mega-unit of penicillin. Another swab showed that the STD had been eliminated.

The baby was safely delivered, and my patient herself had not the slightest trouble. They went on to have more children, and twenty years later they were still happily married. She does not know to this day that she once had gonorrhea or that her husband had been unfaithful.

This was the very antithesis of informed consent. Was it the right thing to do in the interests of her peace of mind and the stability of her marriage?

Problem Case No. 2

When I first started out in practice, it was not uncommon to find that the patient had an unruptured hymen. Now it is the rarest thing, thanks to tampon usage and promiscuity. Sometimes an unmarried girl would be pregnant with an intact hymen, showing that there had been no penetration but the sperm cells had invaded the reproductive tract via the copious ovulatory type of cervical mucus. After a few years I was able to report a series of 30 cases of unconsummated marriage,[4] the purpose being to advocate surgical correction instead of other less successful approaches.

One patient came with a minor gynecological problem at age 50. She had had no children, and had not seen a physician about the problem. Examination showed that the hymen was intact.

I said to her that the obvious reason for her not having conceived was that there had never been penetration. Many patients have painful attempts at intercourse, but do not realize the essence of the problem and the fact that it could easily be remedied. A month later her husband unexpectedly committed suicide. Was he possibly impotent, and now the moment of truth had been forced on them both? Was there remorse on both sides?

Was it my fault? If "speech is silver but silence is golden," would it not have been better to have said nothing because she was past the age of childbearing?

Professional secrecy

Since the time of Hippocrates, it has been the unquestioned rule that confidentiality is of the essence between doctor and patient. This is a basic obligation in justice. Without it there could be no mutual trust; moreover, patients have the right to expect that their secrets will not be revealed.

Doctors are well advised not to discuss anything about patients, however inconsequential, with their wives or staff. It is better to be over-cautious in this matter than to restrict secrecy to more serious matters.

"Didn't your husband tell you I'm pregnant again?"

"No, he never tells me anything."

"Good," thinks the patient, "I can trust him in other things."

Scientific research depends on facts and information, but sometimes the patient's interests take precedence over medical recording. Making notes of every detail about the patient can become an obsession, and it can sometimes work to her disadvantage.

For example, after a patient has had a normal pregnancy and delivery, there is no need to record on each and every subsequent hospital admission that she originally had an induced abortion, whether criminal or legal (what's the difference?). This is now in the past; it obviously has had no sequelae, whether sterility, prematurity, or rupture of the uterus resulting from an abortion perforation. This kind of information can be deleted from the records and the patient advised not to mention it again.

Is the obligation to secrecy absolute? No. It is not like the seal of the confessional, which may never be broken in any circumstances. In the case of medical secrecy, the interests of other members of society sometimes take precedence over those of the patient. In order to protect others, for example, some infectious diseases must be disclosed to the public health authority. For example, a food handler with typhoid might cause an epidemic and many deaths. Those with sexually transmitted diseases of any variety might spread their infections to others, even to children, hence the legal requirement in many places to disclose the names of their partners so that these may be properly notified and take measures to safeguard their health. Leprosy and tuberculosis used to require being quarantined; though that is rarely the case today, these highly contagious diseases require lengthy supervised ongoing treatment, and persons who come into frequent contact with individuals so infected should be properly warned and told how to take the necessary precautions lest they become infected too.

AIDS (Auto Immune Deficiency Syndrome) is a very special case in point. Everyone infected with it will eventually die. Persons who are HIV-positive (who have the human immunovirus) or have full-blown AIDS or ARC (AIDS-related condition), have a serious moral obligation to refrain from any and all activity which might contribute to the spread of this disease: exchange of needles among drug users, sexual activity with same or other-sex partners, etc. They should also advise their partners of the possibility of their having been infected so that they can seek immediate testing and medical care if necessary.

Another dilemma often faces the physician when one of his

patients who works in the transport industry as a bus driver, a truck driver, a train engineer, an airline pilot, a sea captain, etc. is ill with epilepsy, diabetes, a serious heart condition, brain pathology and the like where others' lives are at stake. The first step should be to persuade the patient to reveal the truth of the matter to his employer. If he refuses to do so, the doctor may then approach the local medical authority who may in turn have to proceed to legal means of persuasion.

Has the State the right to set up a Cancer Registry and in the interests of research oblige every such patient to be listed on its computer? It would be quite proper for the patient to refuse cooperation in such a project because his pathology is not placing anyone else at risk and he might have a good reason for wanting privacy. His career might depend on it.

Salus populi suprema lex. The health of the people is the supreme law; or, put in another way, public health comes first. This ancient maxim has much validity, but it is not absolute.

Who owns the medical records?

"I'm moving to another town, Doctor. May I have my records, please?"

Only if the information in them is harmless and non-specific. It would be imprudent if the patient were to read that the doctor suspected that the patient was schizophrenic; or a drug addict; or an alcoholic; or that he had found that she had two episiotomy scars when her husband believed this was her first baby.

Doctors are generally only too willing to cooperate in making all useful information available in these cases. However, there should be no doubt that the records belong to the doctor; they are his *aide mémoire*; they are about the patient but she has no claim to them. His notes are often the only evidence a doctor can offer when and if he is charged with malpractice for having done or omitted to do something important in the care of his patient. The courts may, of course, subpoena these records in civil cases under certain circumstances, and the doctor would be obliged to surrender them.

Unnecessary operations

It is unethical and immoral to operate without a genuine clinical indication; but medicine is not an exact science and therefore in any individual case it is difficult to state that the operation was not justified. However, there is no doubt that the overall picture of the surgical world gives the impression that many operations are performed for inadequate or spurious reasons, and without any discernible benefits to health. In the OB/GYN field, hysterectomy is a prime example of this *furor operandi* (craze for operating). A study from the Dartmouth Medical School in New Hampshire, for example, found that in Maine only 20 percent of women over 70 had had the operation, while in other parts of the United States the hysterectomy incidence was as high as 70 percent.[5]

Mutilating operations

Every operation should have an adequate medical reason to justify its performance, but when it comes to psychological factors the decision becomes more difficult. It has been reported that a lady has had her right breast removed because it was interfering with her golf swing. (Shades of the Amazons of Scythia c. 700 B.C. who were believed to have had one breast removed because it restricted the sword arm!)

In Islamic countries where mutilation is the penalty for some crimes a doctor might be asked to amputate the hand of a thief, but fortunately the *Declaration of Tokyo* does something to protect him now from such pressures.

"Sex change" operations are a modern phenomenon which presents the surgeon with an ethical problem. Usually a man comes to the conclusion that he "is a woman locked up in a man's body" and he wants to become a girl. So he persuades a surgeon to amputate his penis, remove his testicles, fashion some sort of vaginal pouch out of the empty scrotum, and enlarge his breasts by prescribing huge doses of estrogen.

At the end of all this he may look like a woman but he is still the person he always was; he still has to shave every day, his voice is still deep, and the psychological disturbance which led to his initial request still persists, even if temporarily modified. It is futile to try to adjust the body to fit the mind.

If it is a lady who wishes to have the reverse procedure and masquerade as a man, she has to submit to removal of the uterus, ovaries and breasts, and then have a plastic operation to fashion a soft-tissue stump as a pseudo-penis. Besides this, she has to take a constant dose of androgen hormones.

It is interesting to note that the Johns Hopkins Hospital in Baltimore, where these operations were first performed, later gave up the project.[6]

There is no doubt that these gross forms of mutilation are unethical. The Commandment, "Thou shalt not kill" forbids not only homicide and suicide but also mutilation and careless risks to health. On the other hand, other common plastic surgical cosmetic operations which alter the contours of soft tissues or bones are obviously justified for most physical and even certain psychological indications.

Mass medication

Has the state the right to administer medicines or vaccinations to the whole population? It would have this right certainly in the face of a catastrophic epidemic such as the plague (the Black Death of the 14th century), but it would be a mistake to assume these powers and institute draconian public health regulations in less urgent medical crises. There is always talk about requiring every school-child to be vaccinated against rubella (German measles) or tuberculosis, poliomyelitis, hepatitis, etc. The motives behind such laws have to do, not only with the health of the individual child, but the welfare of the other children with whom an infected child might come in contact, and this, of course, is commendable. The record of such endeavors, however, does not always inspire confidence. It is not uncommon, for example, for some injected children, admittedly a small number, to develop a high temperature and then have a febrile fit, which itself might be fatal.

The fluoridation of water supplies is another matter of questionable validity. Should the state force medication on citizens who may not want it? The health problem is a minor one (dental caries) and fluoride pills and toothpastes are available in abundance for those who desire to use them.

It may not be long before some totalitarian government somewhere in this world puts progesterone into the water reservoirs to act as a general contraceptive, which would not only be a gross infringement of individual rights but a pharmacological blunder of the first order as well.

Organ transplants

The development of organ transplantation in the past 30 years is truly amazing. Once there was only the relatively simple shaving off of a translucent cornea to replace a scarred cornea in a blind patient; but now whole organs, such as the liver, or groups of organs (heart and lungs) can be transplanted into a recipient's body. The healthy organs come from either a cadaver or from a living donor.

The cadaveric donor is usually considered to be "brain dead" but there are two difficulties, one being the definition of death and the other its precise diagnosis. The transplant surgeon does not want a dead organ; he wants only a living, beating heart. The *Declaration of Sydney* (see p. 25) attempted to furnish guidelines on how surgeons ought to proceed, but the basic problem seems to be incapable of resolution.

If the patient is comatose, the next of kin may give permission for the organ removal; the living donor gives his or her own assent. In the latter case it is usually a matter of using one of paired organs, such as the kidneys. The "physiological reserve" of these organs is sufficient to keep the donor going in good health with only one kidney.

Dazzled by the brilliance of the surgical technique and the restoration to health of a young patient in renal failure, we seldom ask the fundamental questions. Is it right to give one's organs, or to receive another person's organs? Is it prudent? Does a sibling have a duty to donate an organ to a seriously ill brother or sister for whom they may be a perfect match?

There is no doubt that it is licit, even an admirable act of charity, to give one's organs, if not one's life, for a friend. Whether it is prudent is another question. The aim of the exercise is to cheat death, to prolong life for some indefinite time, perhaps a few years in younger patients, sometimes only days in older ones.

It is unfair to pressure young siblings to donate, say, bone marrow or a kidney because of the risks of anesthesia and operation, and the fact that the loss of the organ might be regretted in the future. In my own city recently, a healthy donor died from operative complications after giving a kidney to his impaired brother. One way of minimizing, if not completely avoiding, this heartbreaking decision is to require anonymity when several family members are being tested for tissue compatibility with the aim of reducing rejection reactions. But the decision to give assent must be faced eventually.

With the advances in microsurgery of blood vessels, it is only a matter of time before ovarian and testicular transplants become possible. If the purpose of the exercise were solely to make up for the deficiency of the female or male hormones, the operation would be licit. But if it were a matter of accepting the donor's ova or sperm cells, it would be a different matter altogether. This would be illicit, because the genetic material involved is forever bound only to the original marriage partners. Such a transplant would be similar to artificial insemination by a donor, which is a breach of the exclusive nature of marriage and childbearing. Hormones are nonspecific, but genes are of fundamental significance to the partners and to society.

Transplants from the fetus

Are the supporters of legal abortion surprised at the great increase in the use of fetal tissues or organs for transplants or other commercial purposes? Here is a perfect child, the victim of a late abortion. The mother obviously does not want it. Why throw it away with the garbage when it could be used to help a sick patient or to make a small profit on the side? There is already an established trade in fetal fat to make high-grade cosmetic creams. "California Beauty," for example, was a facial cream produced by René Ibry, Inc. and advertised as "exclusively taken from fetuses."[7] Further examples of this identical barbarity are noted in my earlier book.[8]

The anencephalic fetus is a treasure trove for transplant enthusiasts. It has no skull; the upper part of the brain (cerebrum) is undeveloped; the lower part is exposed. The child lives for only a few hours after birth, but the rest of its organs are perfect and are readily available for "harvesting" as it is called — kidneys, heart, lungs, pancreas, corneas. Waiting for an assurance of death becomes an academic gesture.

But she (it is usually a female) is our sister in the human family, despite her gross abnormality. She may look repulsive but she has a right to life, however brief, and to respect. And she has a perfect soul which will soon be in Paradise, along with the Good Thief and many other unlikely candidates.

Probably the most common use of fetal tissue at present is the transplanting of brain material from fresh abortions into patients with Parkinson's Disease (partial generalized paralysis and tremor). The cerebral tissue is minced and injected into the adult patient's brain in the hope that it will produce dopamine, which will in turn reduce the tremor and other neurological symptoms. Some cases have reported benefit but for the majority the exercise has been disappointing, even dangerous.

Another almost unbelievable suggestion was that a woman with kidney failure should become pregnant and then have a late abortion. Her baby's kidneys would then be transplanted into her own body, the rationale being that her own child would be the donor least likely to provoke a rejection phenomenon. This is the ultimate in cruelty and injustice. It is the surgical equivalent of cannibalism.

CHAPTER 5

DEATH, DYING AND EUTHANASIA

Acceptance of Death

Death is the culmination of life, the last great adventure. If we die well, our lives have been successful; if badly, we have been failures. To die well is to be at peace with God, with ourselves and with our fellow man.

Acceptance is the key to illness and to death. "Thy will be done" (Luke 22:42). This was Christ's example at the end of His life. His final prayer He took from the Psalms: "Into Thy hands I commend My spirit" (Psalm 31:5). It would be fitting if we could make it our own, unless we happen to be comatose (how frustrating!), in which case we hope our family will say it for us.

We are all instinctively afraid not of death so much as of the dying process. Courageous souls welcome death because they know they are going home. "My soul is longing and yearning, is yearning for the courts of the Lord" (Psalm 83:3).

Dr. Elisabeth Kubler-Ross is the world authority on the stages of terminal grief, but many patients do not react with her "anger and disbelief." They know that God gives life and only He decides on the time of death. Many doctors find this hard to accept. They themselves want to determine the timing of death, based largely on their own philosophy of life, on the economics of the illness and on the importunings of the relatives.

If a patient dies after a prolonged coma this is often regarded as a mistaken management of the case, but it should rather be seen as a triumph of nursing and medicine. The patient has been given ordinary care, but his going has not been hastened nor has his human dignity been violated. He has not been described as "a vegetable," an insulting and unfortunate reference to "having a vegetative existence," lacking the normal functioning of his autonomic nervous system. Moreover, the respect and patience shown to him increases our confidence in the doctors and nurses when we come, perhaps too soon, to our own last illness.

Patients in coma or disabled

Those suffering from chronic illness (mainly low grade malignancies, degenerative diseases, cerebral deterioration, senility, Alzheimer's Disease, various forms of retardation) present a major problem for nursing and medical services and, with the ageing of the population, this will become worse. It is not really that there are too many old people; rather, there are too few young ones to care for them, thanks to the dramatic fall in the birth rate which is a direct effect of society's anti-natalist philosophy. Those who in their young years promote contraception, sterilization and abortion are digging their own geriatric graves. The policy of sterile sex has reduced the average family to fewer than two children (1.8 statistically). Little wonder that so many people, as they pass into the twilight of their lives, find themselves so lonely and abandoned.

Despite this, one can only feel admiration for the devotion with which young nurses, some not much more than teenagers, care for the elderly and unrewarding patients. Sooner or later the questions arise: how much care should they be given? Should euthanasia be considered?

These problems present themselves in their most acute and difficult form when the patient lies in prolonged coma. The dramatic advances in intensive care have produced patients who can be kept alive but comatose for weeks, months, even years. Ultimately the decision must be made as to whether one should "pull the plug" and disconnect the respirator.

Types of coma

Strange to say, the best analysis of this clinical problem that the average person could wish to read comes not from doctors but from a statement of the Catholic Bishops of Pennsylvania, headed by Cardinal Anthony J. Bevilacqua.[1] The bishops of the State were concerned about recent State and Federal Court decisions dealing with "advanced medical directives," mainly with the so-called "living will" or "durable power of attorney"; and they pointed out that what the civil law allows is not necessarily morally acceptable.

They listed four states of unconsciousness which are usually incorrectly lumped together under the common heading of "coma."

(1) *True coma* — there is no response to stimuli. The patient is asleep, not dead. This state is never permanent; he may awaken after many weeks or he may deteriorate further.

(2) *Persistent vegetative state (PVS)* — there is deep unconsciousness, but some reflex responses. The upper part of the brain (cortex) is impaired but the brainstem is functioning. This is often called "brain dead" but that description is inaccurate.

(3) *Psychiatric pseudo-coma* — unconsciousness caused by shock or trauma. It has a psychological cause.

(4) *Locked-in state* — the descending motor pathways in the nervous system are interrupted, the patient is conscious but is unable to move and gives the impression of being comatose.

In all these comatose states the patient is not dead; he will probably recover except in the PVS which, therefore, poses the most difficult decisions about management.

Ethical principles

We have a duty to care for all patients, however distasteful this may be, whatever the prognosis (long or short), whether or not their problem is self-induced. We are obliged to give *ordinary* but not *extraordinary* care — this is the simplest statement of our obligation. The practical difficulty lies in defining what is ordinary and what is extraordinary.

Ordinary care is obligatory; extraordinary is optional. Ordinary care is limited to basic bed nursing, provision of food and drink, cleanliness, supervision of excretory functions, offering a happy environment of disinterested love, and ensuring that the spiritual needs of the patient are addressed to the extent that this is possible.

Extraordinary care is anything more than that — prolonged intravenous fluids, expensive medications, surgical procedures, using permanent life-support systems, and so forth.

It is impossible to define these obligations with any precision, because the patient's circumstances change from day to day. If what we regard as something more than basic "ordinary" care becomes too painful, or burdensome, or expensive it may be discontinued. Medicine is not an exact science. The major problems lie with those in a Permanent Vegetative State (PVS) or on life-support.

For these PVS patients we can never ignore our duty to provide nutrition and fluids, even if this is through a nasogastric tube (a tube passed down the nose into the stomach and left permanently in place for those who cannot swallow); or through a gastrostomy tube (inserted through the skin directly into the stomach). This is basic ordinary treatment which is not burdensome for either the patient or the nurses. On the other hand, there would be no obligation to operate and create a gastrostomy in a new PVS patient.

The decision to "pull the plug" on PVS or life-support patients is in the news more frequently with each passing year. The most famous case in the United States was that of Karen Ann Quinlan who became comatose after taking drink and drugs in 1975. Her life-support was stopped in 1976 and, to show how inexact the medical assessment can be, she survived, still comatose, until 1980. The parents had asked for her to be removed from the respirator because its continued use seemed pointless and expensive, but the medical staff refused to agree. In these cases there is always the fear that the doctors might be charged with homicide. It was left for the Court to decide, and the judge advised that the parents had the right to seek or refuse this extraordinary treatment. Doctors have no authority over patients; their role is merely that of medical advisors. The patient (or if she is incompetent, her parents, spouse or guardian) has the right to refuse treatment.

A similar case, but with one important difference, was that of Tony Bland in Britain. He had been crushed in a football riot, suffered some form of cerebral accident, and for three and a half years had been in Airedale Hospital permanently comatose in a PVS. He had been kept alive by food and fluids administered through a permanent nasogastric feeding tube. The medical staff considered that removing the tube would be a form of homicide, but the parents petitioned the Court for permission to remove it. Their plea went to the House of Lords and in 1993 five law Lords created a landmark legal precedent by authorizing the removal of the tube. The young man died of starvation in a couple of weeks.

Ethically, Their Lordships were in error. This was obviously a discontinuing of ordinary care. Starving a patient to death has no place in medicine, but now we can expect to see it more frequently. It is already not uncommon in the case of newborn babies with some serious abnormalities.

Doctors are quite capable of making the decision when to

discontinue extraordinary care. To show that the problem is not a new one, see the often quoted couplet of A.H. Clough (d. 1861) in "The Latest Decalogue":

> "Thou shalt not kill; but equally thou shalt not strive
> Officiously to keep alive."

This may be good advice, but the word "officiously" is hypercritical. A better choice would be "unreasonably."

Case Report

I once had a patient who was a spastic, the condition affecting all four limbs, her trunk and face. She could do nothing for herself apart from a messy sort of feeding. Her speech was slow and often unintelligible. With her limbs constantly moving, her face grimacing and salivating, she was not a pretty sight. But the Sisters of Mercy cared for her uncomplainingly for about 20 years. When she was about 40 years of age, someone had the idea of buying her a simple typewriter, and she proceeded to tap out sentences laboriously with a peg in her swaying hand. What she wrote was amazing. Locked up in her frustrated mind had been beautiful thoughts, prayers and stories.

She was 45 when we accidentally discovered that she had a huge fibroid in the uterus which called for a hysterectomy. When she was anesthetized, the spasticity in her limbs suddenly vanished and she looked at peace. She died at about 50 after an apparently faultless life and is now probably enjoying her reward in Heaven. This was the ideal of nursing — ordinary care, endless patience, and an assurance to all the other sick people that this noble love would be available to them when they became disabled in the future.

N.T.B.R.

A growing and obnoxious custom is emerging of annotating certain patients' hospital records as "N.T.B.R." (not to be resuscitated). In the United States, N.T.B.R. is called D.N.R.: do not resuscitate. This is intended to dissuade the staff from treating these sick patients when they eventually collapse, but it is insulting to label them in this cold-blooded fashion. Moreover, it offends against the fundamental medical principle that the clinician in charge of the patient at that time, junior or senior, must accept full responsibility for his decisions. It is also dangerous because the initial diagnosis might be inaccurate, and therefore a treatable condition may be overlooked. This is analogous to the "living will" by which the patient seeks to constrain any future physician. The testator does not realize what she is signing. She would be better advised to leave the day to day decisions about the management of her last illness to the common sense of her doctor.

Euthanasia

We live in a world of euphemisms. Euthanasia etymologically means "easy death," and who could possibly quarrel with that? But euphemisms aim to hide unpleasant facts and obscure the truth. And however nicely "euthanasia" is promoted in society, nothing can obscure the fact that it is for the patient *suicide* and for the doctor *homicide*. It is called "death with dignity" but there is not dignity in either suicide or homicide.

Will the medical profession have enough courage and nobility to resist this subversion of its fundamental ethic? Hippocrates refused to countenance euthanasia. The Christian tradition has always rejected suicide, as witness Shakespeare's heroine, Imogen, who was considering suicide when her husband, Leonatus, had mistakenly ordered her murder:

"Against self-slaughter there is a prohibition so divine
That cravens my weak hand." (*Cymbeline*, III, iv, 78)

The growth of euthanasia societies in the past few years is extraordinary — but is it surprising that nations which approve of abortion for the abnormal fetus soon progress to the elimination of the abnormal adult? The first meeting of the World Federation of Right to Die Societies was held in Tokyo in 1976. Later meetings were in San Francisco (1978), Oxford (1980), Melbourne (1982), Nice (1984) and now they are more frequent and more strongly supported. At the Nice meeting Christiaan Barnard, the pioneer South African cardiac surgeon, openly agreed that it is illogical to permit abortion and at the same time to forbid the killing of the terminally ill. In his book[2] he revealed that he had applied passive euthanasia to his own mother; and he has a euthanasia/suicide pact with his brother.

A most peculiar phenomenon is observed in the Netherlands, which 40 years ago was a staunchly Catholic country but has, since the Second Vatican Council, been in serious disagreement with Rome over a number of doctrinal and moral issues. During the same period of time, the euthanasia movement has flourished there as nowhere else. The leading Dutch protagonist is Dr. Pieter Admiraal, who claims that some 20,000 patients are dispatched by mercy-killing doctors and nurses each year, and it is commonly believed that many of the victims have not given their consent to this "treatment."

It is difficult to credit these figures. Considering the common causes of death — infant deaths, accidents, cardiac failure, cancer, degenerative diseases, infections, etc. — it is impossible to believe that, of the 120,000 total annual deaths, about one sixth of the patients need be considered for euthanasia. One wonders whether the problem lies more with the doctors and nurses than with the patients.

It is well recognized that nurses who turn their hand to dispatching the elderly easily become obsessed with it and earn the title of "Angels of Death." In 1988 a Dutch nurse was charged with killing 23 of her geriatric patients. A German nurse, Michaele Roeder, in 1989 was accused of performing a similar service for 17 patients. Also in 1989, three nurses in the Lainz Hospital, Vienna, were arrested for killing some 35 patients by lethal injection. Blood lust is a very real psychological phenomenon. Once the first killing is over, the others seem to follow with an air of inevitability.

The need for caution is obvious, but a recent opinion poll showed that 80 percent of the Dutch people approve of voluntary euthanasia. In 1993 the Dutch Parliament by a majority of 91 to 45 passed a permissive law which virtually guaranteed doctors immunity when they applied euthanasia to their patients. The Justice Minister, Mr. Hirsch-Ballin, hoped that "the new law would bring mercy killing out into the open where it can be properly regulated." How often have we heard these pious hopes, and how often have they been proved wrong. Various countries have legislated to "regulate" prostitution, abortion, homosexuality, alcoholism, drug addiction — and they have always failed.

Throughout the world there is an upsurge of support for legalized euthanasia, attributable partly to the prevailing "culture of death," to the decline in religious belief and practice, and also to unrealistic fears about how distressing the dying process might be. It is only a minority of patients who suffer significantly at this time; and indeed the worldwide hospice movement has demonstrated how easeful dying can be if it is properly managed.

Meanwhile, at the time of this writing, Dr. Jack Kevorkian, a retired pathologist from the State of Michigan in the United States, is seeking fame, or notoriety, by flagrantly publicizing a succession of deaths which he has brought about, in contravention of State law, by means of a "suicide machine" which he has invented. He now has an impressive tally of "assisted suicides" in the United States and Canada and has no plans to curtail his activity in this area at all.

Ethical assessment

The basic ethical principle is that *suicide* and *homicide*, which exist reciprocally in euthanasia, are serious moral faults and no circumstances can justify them. They are forbidden by the Commandment, "Thou shalt not kill." This, as one hardly needs to stress, is not a Roman Catholic law or even simply a Jewish prohibition. It was given by God to all humanity, and it has always been interpreted as "Thou shalt not kill the innocent."

Euthanasia operates in two forms, *active* or *passive*.

Active euthanasia means direct killing, either by the common technique of drug overdose or by lethal injection (usually intravenous). If the patient is the initiator, it is suicide; if the doctor, homicide.

Passive euthanasia is simply withholding food and drink or some essential medication. In the former the patient is literally starved to death — a slow form of death but indirect homicide nevertheless. This is the common management of PVS patients in some hospitals. The medical and nursing staffs tire of their seemingly unrewarding care; the hospital management complains about the apparent waste of money; and the family find themselves physically and emotionally drained and some may even see their inheritance trickling away in drip feeding.

In an authoritative but brief review of the euthanasia crisis, Msgr. William B. Smith confirmed the validity of the concepts of "ordinary" and "extraordinary" care; or, as he put it, ordinary means obligatory and extraordinary means optional. Depriving patients of food and fluids can by no stretch of the imagination be regarded as extraordinary care. No circumstances justify this dereliction of nursing and medical duty.[3]

The fact that the patient has asked for death does not make the fateful deed licit. Hippocrates 24 centuries ago commented on the same dilemma: "I will give no deadly medicine to anyone if asked, nor suggest any such counsel." Not only would this be wrong from a moral point of view, it would also destroy the confidence that patients have in doctors if they knew that euthanasia was an option in their case.

Magisterial statements

"I have set before you a choice," God tells us in the Book of Deuteronomy (30:19), "a choice between life or death, a blessing or a curse . . . Choose life that you may live!" In the matter of abortion and euthanasia, society and the medical profession are more and more often opting for death which will bring upon the world not a blessing but a curse.

From an address of Pope John Paul II to Working Groups of the Pontifical Academy of Sciences, October 21, 1985, on the subject of euthanasia we read:

"Scientists and physicians are called to place their skill and energy at the service of life. They can never, for any reason or in any case, extinguish it . . . (E)uthanasia is a crime in which one must in no way cooperate or even consent to. Scientists and physicians must not regard themselves as the lords of life but as its skilled and generous servants."

The main magisterial teachings which he quotes are: Pope Pius XII in "Prolongation of Life," 1957; the Vatican "Declaration on Euthanasia" issued by the Congregation for the Doctrine of the Faith, 1980; and "The Ethical and Religious Directives for Catholic Health Facilities" written by the National Conference of (American) Catholic Bishops, 1975. In this the bishops state:

"Euthanasia (mercy killing) in all its forms is forbidden. The failure to supply the ordinary means of preserving life is equivalent to euthanasia. However, neither the physician nor the patient is obliged to use extraordinary means."

The new dilemma in modern medicine stems from several similar court decisions, notably the Bouvia case in California, which direct doctors and nurses to discontinue even the minimal means of life preservation, namely, food, water, bed nursing and personal hygiene. In these the courts have exceeded their authority and have made decisions which are *ultra vires*. It is in the care of the terminally ill that nursing achieves its noblest ideals and performs services which doctors could not possibly equal — the obligation of basic human care.

CHAPTER 6

THE ABNORMAL, THE UNWANTED

The role of the abnormal

Few things are more admirable than the medical and nursing care that is given to abnormal adults and children in thousands of homes and hospitals throughout the world. This is the acme of Christian charity. The patients often cannot respond or express appreciation to their attendants; they need endless patience; their prognosis is usually hopeless; but they are treated with love and respect for their injured human dignity. When justice is afforded to these most defenceless of the poor, all our lives are safe. But when we begin to denigrate, abuse and abandon them to their fate as the Nazis did when they began liquidating those "useless eaters" (as Hitler called them), the life of every human being is immediately placed at risk.

It is obvious that the role of the abnormal in society is not clearly appreciated. They serve indirectly to highlight the beauty of the normal which, but for them, might not be properly valued. Christ providentially taught us that lesson in the story of the man born blind. People asked Him if the blindness was a penalty for the sins of either the man or his parents, but He replied: "He was born blind so that the works of God might be revealed through him" (Jn 9:3). Quite apart from his miraculous cure there was the fact that, if there was no such thing as blindness, we would never realize what a wonderful gift sight is for us.

The abnormal child

Most of the ethical problems center on these poor creatures which society often looks upon as pathetic discards. Down's Syndrome (Mongolism or Trisomy-21) babies are a common challenge to the medical profession. They are often born with another associated abnormality such as a cardiac defect or duodenal atresia (blockage of the first part of the small bowel). Should they be operated on? On the one hand, most people feel that an operation should not be denied to a patient simply because of the presence of some other pathology. On the other hand, surgeons will often be unwilling to undertake a prolonged and difficult operation when the patient might have other abnormalities or a limited life expectancy. But without an operation, the child might be unable to eat and drink normally and he will die within a couple of weeks. It is impossible to work out a simple formula that will resolve this dilemma in every case. It is easy to say: Operate on every case. But this might not always be the most prudent policy. Cases must be decided on an individual basis, one by one.

Baby Doe

In the United States in 1983, the President set up a Commission for the Study of Ethical Problems in Medicine and Biomedical and Behavioral Research. One of its Reports was on "Deciding to Forego Life-sustaining Treatment"; this was partly based on the "Baby Doe" case which at that time created a precedent. This Down's Syndrome child had a tracheo-esophageal fistula, an open communication between the main airway and the gullet. When he drank milk, it was diverted into the lungs. Repairing the fistula is a major operation for a one-day-old child, because the thorax has to be opened and the risk of a fatal outcome in such cases is not inconsiderable.

The parents opted for avoidance of surgery, but the hospital authorities took the case to Court. The judge agreed that the decision of the parents was within their rights, and that the medical staff had no authority to force their will in this matter, however sad and frustrating that might appear to be.

If it were a simpler bowel obstruction problem that could be remedied by a 10-minute abdominal operation (gastroenterostomy) would the parents have been obliged to authorize that? No one can give a universal answer. All that one can state is that basic fluids and nutrition may not be withheld — but in these cases the food intake is soon vomited up again.

Another case

A relatively new phenomenon in medicine and nursing is allowing babies with spina bifida to starve to death, perhaps assisted with heavy sedation. These children have a defect in the lower spinal column covered with a cystic swelling on the skin. The legs and bladder are paralyzed; they have to live in a wheelchair, but their intelligence is normal and they often have happy, endearing natures.

In 1986 in Melbourne, Australia, there was just such a case where the parents agreed to the starvation regimen. After two days, the grandparents applied to the Supreme Court seeking its legal protection. In a landmark decision, Mr. Justice Vincent ordered the hospital to commence feeding the child.

"No parent," he said, "no doctor, no court has any power to determine that the life of any child, however disabled the child may be, will be deliberately taken from it. I want this proposition very clearly understood by all concerned." He warned that any course of medical treatment deliberately chosen for the purpose of bringing about the death of a child is unlawful and it could result in "criminal charges of a most serious kind."

In 1984, the American Academy of Pediatrics had also made a reassuring statement on this issue: "Discrimination of any type against any individual with a disability, regardless of the nature or severity of the disability, is morally and legally indefensible."

Wanted or unwanted?

The modern child, and particularly the abnormal child, suffers the risk of being labelled "unwanted," therefore not worth treating, therefore disposable through abortion or infanticide. Married partners often hold the unreasonable view that they are entitled to perfect offspring, and that anything abnormal is not part of the contract or their expectations. If the unborn child is described as "unwanted," it immediately becomes fair game for the abortionists. This philosophy is fostered by the Family Planning Association which has as its motto: "Every child a wanted child!" Such a concept is, of course, completely spurious. Every child has from God certain basic human rights — the right to life; and the right to be wanted and loved by its parents.

It is a dereliction of duty for parents to reject their own child and call it "unwanted." It is sentimental and short-sighted, and for the medical attendants to take such a statement seriously is generally naive. It is very common for the patient to state in early pregnancy when she is sick, tired and depressed that the child is unwanted, but in 99 percent of the cases when it is born she smiles and holds it and hugs it and gives it a big welcome. She wouldn't let you take it from her for all the world.

Sex selection of children

While most parents' attempts to have a boy or a girl by timing intercourse either at or before ovulation can be regarded as more of an entertaining gamble than anything else, the fact remains that in some circumstances sex selection can have sinister overtones.

In Communist China where the irrational one-child family is enforced by legislation, the parents have a strong preference for male babies, not only for cultural reasons but also because the boys are an investment in their future security. Therefore antenatal diagnosis of the sex of the fetus takes on new importance for them. This is achieved by either amniocentesis or chorionic villus sampling (CVS). The former draws off some of the liquor in which the baby moves, usually at about 18 weeks maturity, and the cells shed into the liquid give the diagnosis. CVS is performed by a long needle at about 10 weeks and has the advantage of an earlier diagnosis.

Both techniques have an alarming complication of accidental miscarriage. And, if the wrong sex is diagnosed, there is a high incidence of induced abortion. In England there have been cases of such abortions in families which are burdened with hereditary titles. Lord Jones naturally wants a little boy to be the next Lord Jones, not a little girl to be a simple Honorable Miss Jones, so the latter finds herself aborted simply for being the wrong sex. The technique is used also in cases of sex-linked hereditary diseases such as hemophilia, which is transmitted by the females but affects only the males. Which sex should be attacked? Usually it is the ill-fated males who are eliminated.

The latest development is sex selection before conception, based on the experiments of Professor Tizuka of Keio University, Japan. He devised a technique of separating the X-chromosome (female) sperms from the Y-chromosome (male) sperms by centrifuging. At present those practicing this arcane specialty claim about 75 percent accuracy in achieving the desired sex. The husband produces the semen by masturbation, and after centrifuging the semen, the wife is artificially inseminated with the appropriate sperms. Both of these procedures are morally unacceptable. Ejaculation and the mutual transfer of the germ cells must take place only during the normal loving marital embrace.

Ethical assessment

Donald De Marco, Ph.D.,[1] points out that spouses have the right to marital intercourse but they cannot demand the right to fertility or to sex selection. "The attempt to determine the sex of one's child is incompatible with the reverence that is appropriate for the proper conferring and receiving of both these gifts" (that is, the gift of life and that of gender).

This, sad to say, is just one more example of the modern phenomenon of regarding children as chattels, something to fulfill the desires of one or both of the parents, to make them happy, to tidy up the family structure, or to make doctors proud of their ingenious technical advances.

In every country where sex selection is practiced, the choice of the parents in the great majority of cases is for boy babies. This is an insult to women. And at the same time it can produce a serious imbalance in the future sex ratios in society. Militant feminists are therefore in a cleft stick of their own making — they have advocated sexual freedom and abortion on demand, and this results in an unjust discrimination against females. Any departure from divine law places all human beings, but especially females in these cases, at risk.

CHAPTER 7

REPRODUCTIVE SYSTEM

Ethical problems in sexuality

Most of the ethical problems in modern medicine center on the reproductive system because of its unique nature. It deals with life and the sources of life, therefore it is of major importance to individuals, to marriage, to society and to the future of the nation. When we devote so much space to it, we should not be accused of having a kink about sex. It is just that sexual activities are so basic, that faults in this area are the common lot of mankind, and that the medical profession is now deeply involved in many aspects of sexuality, more often than not with disastrous results.

The discussion will deal mainly with ethical problems in sexuality, but it will be impossible to avoid some brief reference to clinical, sociological and demographic aspects of the subject.

Sexual philosophy must necessarily be a consistent and integrated whole. We cannot pick and choose in an eclectic fashion some modern approaches which appeal to us and reject the rest. If we are not wholly right we will find ourselves being wholly wrong. There appears to be a syndrome of sexual abnormality and, if we diagnose one or two facets of it, we can be certain that ultimately the whole of the underlying social malaise will reveal itself.

A fatal progression

This is illustrated by the modern observation that there is *an inevitable progression* from contraception to sterilization and finally to abortion and euthanasia. Within the past 40 years, history has proved this true — in society as a whole and in the medical profession specifically. Within living memory there was initially the reluctant acceptance of contraception and then an explosive increase in its use from the time of the introduction of "the pill" (oral contraception) in 1960. Following this there was a slow move to sterilization and finally a frenetic embracing of worldwide abortion which is now a juggernaut that nothing can stop. It crushes beneath its wheels some 50 million unborn children every year. In an atmosphere where all life has become dispensable, the number of people who will eventually fall victim to euthanasia can only be imagined with horror.

The facts contradict the conventional wisdom which holds that more contraception will lead to fewer abortions. The reality is, especially among the young and unmarried, that the use of contraception has led to a greater frequency in the incidence of sexual intercourse and hence to more pregnancies and, ultimately, more abortions.

This underscores the heavy responsibility which rests on those who promote contraception. To quote a homely example of the real and unholy alliance between contraception and abortion, the first abortion clinic in my city was dedicated to the memory of none other than the local founder of the Family Planning Association. And the former President of the Family Planning Association was recently promoted to be President of — guess what — the Abortion Law Reform Association.

Mary Pride is an evangelical Christian who was once a militant feminist. She says: "Feminism is a totally consistent system aimed at rejecting God's role for women." And with unusual insight she confirms the claims made above: "Family planning is the mother of abortion. A generation had to be indoctrinated in the ideal of planning children around personal convenience before abortion could become popular."[1]

While the average person may have difficulty in seeing the unexpected implications of contraception, the recent Popes who have spoken on this subject did not. With uncanny perception they predicted the evils that would follow; this is true especially of Pius XI in his encyclical, *Casti Connubii* (1930) and Paul VI in *Humanae Vitae* (1968).

The explanation for this fateful progression can be found in society's philosophy of sexuality. In previous centuries, apart from occasional eruptions of Malthusianism, society has in the main been pro-natalist (in favor of births). In the modern world it has become almost totally antinatalist, and this has been so successful that it now threatens the continued existence of many Western countries. Nearly all of them have birth rates well below replacement level. Race suicide has already arrived, and its impact will become more obvious with every passing year. And the medical profession has been one of the main agents in promoting this "culture of death."

Further deterioration

Now a more sinister implication has emerged. The progression from contraception to sterilization to abortion can be further expanded, thanks to the inexorable logic of a philosophy which denies the truth about human sexuality. Once the life-giving purpose of the sex act has been severed from it through contraception, there is no logical reason why one should not accept masturbation and homosexual activity (equally sterile forms of sexual activity). The anti-life syndrome is complete. Bishop Charles Gore foresaw the linkage as long ago as 1930 when the Anglican Lambeth Conference for the first time approved contraception. And in 1990 a homosexual clergyman, Rev. Richard Kirker, General Secretary of the Gay Christian Movement in Britain, stated that if contraception is acceptable, homosexuality must logically be approved. "If [sterile] sex can be valid for the pleasure it gives heterosexuals, gay people can enjoy their form of sex in the same way." This is treated in greater detail in my book, *The Doctor and Christian Marriage*. Confirmation of the concept of a consistent sexual philosophy which puts personal pleasure above responsible love is found in an important book by George Gilder.[2] His main thesis, backed by impressive sociological data, is that the modern sexual scene favors men at the expense of women. With frequent divorce and universal contraception, philandering is made easy for both sexes, but women suffer more.

Great numbers of women end up lonely and financially disadvantaged because they have lost the only real protection women have, namely, monogamous, permanent, heterosexual marriage. Gilder, who has no specific religious affiliation, points out as a side issue that societies which accept sterile sex or which, through polygamy, reduce marriage opportunities for males, always progress to increased homosexuality.

Masturbation

This abuse of the sex act has become extraordinarily widespread, and even been espoused by the medical profession. Sexologists have made big business of it, recommending it to their clients in the vain hope that it will improve their heterosexual performance. Most modern books on marriage and sexuality (with the exception of this one!) seek to reassure readers with endless repetition that masturbation is "normal," that the only harm which may come from it are feelings of guilt, occasioned by Judeo-Christian religious disapproval.[3]

This universal feeling of guilt is an interesting phenomenon. The explanation which blames it on religious disapproval is too facile, though, to account for its persistence. There is something in human nature which is repulsed by that which lowers one in his or her own self esteem and which recognizes in masturbation a surrender to one's less noble impulses for purposes which are hardly praiseworthy.

The main area in which the medical profession overtly supports masturbation is in the investigation of male fertility. The routine is to require a specimen of semen obtained through masturbation. But, as explained in the later section on fertility, this procedure is unnecessary in making the diagnosis and, moreover, it adds nothing to the solving of the couple's problem.

Ethical assessment

Masturbation is always objectively wrong. Whether the person is subjectively culpable depends on several factors, as discussed in Chapter 2. The reproductive system differs from all other bodily systems in that it is designed physiologically for use with a person of the opposite sex — the male for penetration and ejaculation, the female for reception and conception. The fact that it is possible to induce sexual sensations and reactions in a solitary fashion does not make it right.

According to the proto-sexologists, Dr. Kinsey and Drs. Masters and Johnson, masturbation is common, therefore it is "normal," therefore morally right. Because of defects in their investigation, one can doubt that it is as common as they claim, but even if the incidence were 100 percent it would still be wrong because it offends against the natural moral law, the revealed divine law and the constant Judeo-Christian tradition. The Commandments, "Thou shalt not commit adultery" and "Thou shalt not covet thy neighbor's wife" have always been understood to condemn all forms of sexual sin.

These principles were reaffirmed by the *Vatican Declaration on Sexual Morality* (1975) which was promulgated to clarify the teaching on those activities about which people had become confused because of modern propaganda and social trends — masturbation, pre-marital intercourse and homosexual activity. All three are wrong in every circumstance.

Assuming the prerequisites for freedom of decision and of action, masturbation can never be justified. We may therefore not recommend it to our patients as a supposed therapy for their sexual problems; or for investigation of sterility; or as a variation within marriage; or as a licit activity before marriage ("petting").

Similar considerations forbid "oral sex" (fellatio and cunnilingus). If masturbation were to be acceptable, these two activities would have to be welcomed with equal enthusiasm. But they are simply perversions made "acceptable" by the so-called sexual revolution which has caused far more heartache and degradation than one can imagine.

CHAPTER 8

CONTRACEPTION

The spread of contraception

The more precise term for this discussion is, of course, artificial contraception, that is, anything that is done to render the marriage act sterile. This is usually achieved either by altering the nature of intercourse or by deranging, temporarily or permanently, the reproductive mechanism.

With contraception being welcomed by the millions, with its being a billion-dollar business, with most brides and many unmarried teenagers religiously taking their pill every day, who would have the nerve to say that all of this is wrong? The Roman Catholic Church does. And so do a few courageous smaller churches. Yet all the major churches held the same views up till 1930, when the Lambeth Conference for the first time gave its limited and reluctant approval of contraception. Since that time, birth control ("family planning," "responsible parenthood" and other euphemisms) has enjoyed explosive growth. But with the passing years, more and more people are becoming disenchanted with this sexual Midas touch and the illusory joys which it promised. As every broken-hearted mother, every promiscuous teenager and every abandoned wife knows, the current flood of disastrous premarital and extra-marital affairs would not be possible were it not for the assistance of contraception and of the medical profession which provides the service.

As the discussion here is mainly on ethics, this is not the place to detail the medical, social, legal and demographic ill-effects of contraception. These have been dealt with in my book[1] which has been mentioned above. The same applies to the sections on sterilization and abortion.

Ethical assessment

The basic error of contraception is that it divorces the two main elements of marital sex, the life-giving and the love-giving. Or, in other words, the loving and the fertile aspects. These two should normally be given and received by each spouse simultaneously. It is not open to us to seek one aspect (love) and reject the other (fertility), as this would vitiate the divine plan for married love and it would repudiate an essential, if unspoken, obligation under the marriage contract. Note that the obligation is not to achieve pregnancy as often as possible; it is merely that the marriage act must be carried through normally, even if pregnancy is impossible to achieve on this or all occasions of intercourse.

Sex willfully minus fertility may have the appearance of love, but a deliberately chosen sterility is not love and must deteriorate in the long run. Sex minus love is simply lust. In the Creator's plan, sex means both love and fertility. Contraception repudiates one (fertility) but hopes to preserve the other (love).

The importance of preserving simultaneous life-giving and love-giving is highlighted by a consideration of *in vitro* fertilization (IVF). In this technique, the semen is produced by masturbation in one location and the insemination of the wife is performed in another. The whole procedure is manifestly artificial and abnormal, even if a charming baby is the end result. "The end does not justify the means" once again applies in this case.

In addition to the fundamental ethical defect of contraception in general, it is necessary to consider each individual technique and assess its moral quality as judged by the basic marriage virtues of love, justice and purity.

(1) *Barrier methods* — mainly the condom and the diaphragm. These old methods were condemned and rejected by the Family Planning Association when the pill was introduced in 1960, but they are now making a comeback as a prophylaxis against AIDS. As they never stopped pregnancy in the past, and as the head of the spermatozoa is 50 times as large as the less than 1-micron AIDS virus (HIV - human immunovirus), no informed practitioner seriously believes that they will be more than occasionally effective.

Moreover, since the ovum is vulnerable for only one day in each cycle while the AIDS virus is active every day of the month, it is easy to see that the condom, which was never all that effective in preventing pregnancy, will certainly be less so in preventing the spread of the AIDS virus.

The moral assessment of the condom, however, is not made on its efficacy but on what its use involves, namely the deliberate will of the user to separate from the marital act its life-giving potential. The condom transforms the male organ into an indifferent phallus just as the diaphragm converts the female tract into an indifferent cavity. This is made even more obvious in the case of the new female condom (Femidom). Their use offends against the virtue of marital chastity. As George Bernard Shaw once said, their use should really be seen as "mutual masturbation."

(2) *Coitus interruptus* — this is the deliberate withdrawal before ejaculation so that the semen is deposited outside of the vagina. It is the oldest, the simplest, and in many parts of the world probably the most common form of birth control. It was the sin of Onan who "spilled his seed on the ground" because he did not want to have children by his dead brother's widow, something which, under the old Mosaic law, he was obliged to do. And "God slew him because he did a detestable thing" (Genesis 38:8-10). This is the reason that theologians have always used the term "onanism" to cover all forms of contraception.

Coitus interruptus is likewise an offence against marital chastity. If intercourse is embarked on, the act must ordinarily be carried through to its natural completion unless one is impeded from doing so by an unintended and unexpected interruption or an inability to complete the act for some physical or psychological reason. In these cases the interruption is not deliberately willed.

(3) *Hormonal methods* — The main forms of hormonal birth control methods are oral contraceptives (OCs), usually in the form of a small daily dose of estrogen and progesterone, which are taken in a cyclical fashion. There is still some uncertainty about precisely how these hormonal methods work, but we can be fairly sure that they act mainly on the anterior pituitary gland in the brain with consequential suppression of ovulation. They also alter the character of the cervical mucus to make it impenetrable to sperms. The use of hormonal methods to prevent conception in this fashion is a type of sterilization which is medical in nature and usually temporary. Sterilization, as we have seen, is a serious moral fault when done for indications that are other than medical in nature.

Over the years the conviction has been growing that these hormones might also be abortifacient, and if that were so their use would have even more serious implications. The suspicion is based on the observation that ovulation is not suppressed in a minority, but still a significant number, of cycles but still the pregnancy rate is very low. Pregnancy might therefore occur, but the endometrial atrophy caused by the hormones prevents implantation from occurring.

(4) *Spermicidal creams* or pessaries for insertion into the vagina; and also the postcoital douche. These are all sterilizing in action.

(5) *Intrauterine devices* (IUDs). Once again the mode of action of these devices is uncertain, but the strong probability is that they act as abortifacients through preventing implantation of the early pregnancy. Since ovulation occurs normally in these cases, fertilization must be successful in many instances but the impact on the endometrium of the foreign body (causing infection), or of the hormone impregnation of the plastic shapes, or of the chemical reaction from copper wire binding, all create a disruption of the normal early pregnancy events. Another reason for the success of

IUDs is an unrelated and unintended one, namely, the foreign body causes slight intrauterine infection which is sufficient to block the minute cavity of the tubes and therefore the woman, all unaware, would be unable to conceive even if she were using no contraceptive method at all. Another theory is that the IUD interferes with tubal function and prevents the passage of ovum or sperms; but this favors an increase in ectopic pregnancies (in the tube).

Abortifacients, even if operating at an early state in pregnancy, are serious offences against the virtue of justice. But it must be stated that most of the women using IUDs are unaware of the mode of action, and therefore would not be held culpable on this issue.

(6) *Post-conceptional family planning.* As its misleading and euphemistic name so clearly implies, this is not contraception but early abortion, and it stands condemned on those grounds. The main technique is the *"morning-after pill,"* which is a huge dose of estrogen taken in the cold light of dawn after the sexual liaison of the night before. It aims to prevent implantation; but there is a significant failure rate, and some of the pregnancies will be ectopics. If the pregnancy carries on, the unfortunate fetus will have been exposed to a high estrogen environment at this critical early stage of development and, even if it escapes from a teratogenic disaster (fetal malformation), it may suffer from effects later. When estrogens used to be given throughout pregnancy in the (mistaken) management of diabetes, some of the girl children showed up with a previously unrecorded condition, cancer of the vagina some 20 years later.

Another technique under this heading is *"menstrual extraction,"* another semantic prevarication. If the woman is actually pregnant, it is plainly an early abortion.

(7) *Natural family planning,* based on ovulation detection and restriction of intercourse to the infertile days of the cycle. Using this system normal intercourse is preserved, there is no interference with the reproductive mechanism and no suspicion of abortion. It is open to married couples to have intercourse whenever they wish and

to abstain as they wish, even if they know the wife is fertile or infertile at that particular time.

The NFP system is the only one which is ethically unexceptionable. For married couples who wish to live according to right moral principles, the practical conclusion to be drawn is that their choice is limited to NFP. Every other method is morally flawed in some way.

I wrote my first article on NFP almost 40 years ago[2] but even back then my method failure rate was only 3 per 100 woman-years. Since that time there have been great advances and now NFP is as effective as "the pill," if not more so. Ovulation can be detected by several accurate methods — the basal body temperature; ovulation pain (*Mittelschmerz*); changes in the cervical mucus discharge; changes in the cervix itself (it becomes soft, the os opens, and it moves to a higher level in the pelvis); chemical changes in the mucus; changes in the electropotential within the vagina; and so on.

The clinical genius of Hippocrates is astounding. Practicing in the 4th century B.C., he was aware of the changes in the cervix and its discharge! In *Aphorism No. 62* he stated: "Women in whom the cervical os is cold and thick tend not to conceive easily. Similarly a very moist os drowns and destroys the semen while an unusually dry and hot condition destroys the seed from lack of nourishment. Women who are free from these extremes are those who conceive best."[3] He might have some of the deductions back to front but the remarkable thing is his observations on these physiological changes, something of which many doctors with their expensive equipment are often unaware.

As King Solomon (who died about 930 B.C.) observed: "There is nothing new under the sun" (Ecclesiastes 1:9).

It can confidently be asserted that those who live by the physiological NFP system do not progress to sterilization and then to abortion. They also enjoy stable marriages, perhaps the fruit of their practice of marital chastity and of the sexual self-discipline that it requires.

Papal statements

The Popes do not make moral laws; they merely interpret the laws revealed by God through Scripture, the natural law, tradition and the inspiration of the Holy Spirit. The principles they teach may not always be popular, especially in the area of sexuality, but they have ultimately proven to be correct. The present Pope is responsible as head of the Church for some 920 million souls, about 20 percent of the world's population. He and his immediate predecessors foresaw the consequences of a contraception mentality, namely the modern disasters of the so-called sexual revolution, but few others had that insight.

Pope Pius XI in *Casti Connubii* (1930) said: "The Catholic Church, to whom God has Himself committed the integrity and decency of morals, now standing in this ruin of morals, raises her voice aloud though our mouth, in sign of her divine mission, in order to keep the chastity of the nuptial bond free from this evil error, and again promulgates:

"Any use whatever of marriage, in the exercise of which the act by human effort is deprived of its natural power of procreating life, violates the law of God and of nature, and those who do such a thing are stained with a grave and mortal sin."

In his Address to Italian Midwives (1951), Pope Pius XII confirmed this unchangeable principle and answered the objections, which are still being made — namely, that the prohibition of contraception was mainly a cultural thing which was appropriate to past ages but it would have to be dropped in the modern world if the Church wishes to be credible, especially to the young. He said:

"This precept is in force today, as it was yesterday, and will be so tomorrow and always, because it is not a simple injunction of human law but is the expression of both natural law and divine law."

Pope John XXIII did not issue any major statement on this subject, but it is obvious from his allocutions that his teaching was identical with that of his predecessors.

The most dramatic ruling was, of course, that of Pope Paul VI in his encyclical, *Humanae Vitae* (1968). The Pope was unduly tardy in speaking (the leaked "majority report" of his advisory commission had indicated that the prohibition of contraception was about to be lifted to accommodate the millions who had started taking "the pill," and many people expected the Vatican to embrace the position of the FPA), but the Vicar of Christ stood firm. The essence of the teaching is to be found in No. 11:

"Nonetheless the Church, calling men back to the observance of the norms of the natural law, as interpreted by her constant doctrine, teaches that each and every marriage act must remain open to the transmission of life."

That simple statement is the crucial one. Its practical interpretation is that: only normal intercourse is permissible; nothing may be done to alter the act or to wreck the reproductive mechanism; it is not necessary that "life" be achieved, merely that the normal function be preserved. Assuming that the marriage act is embarked on in love, the love-giving and the life-giving aspects will be achieved together.

Pope John Paul II, addressing the Pontifical Council for the Family (1985), stated that the Church teaching on responsible parenthood had been clearly expressed in *Humanae Vitae*, in his own apostolic exhortation on the family (*Familiaris Consortio*), during his many weekly audiences and in pastoral statements by bishops around the world. In spite of this, "disorientation and doubt" continue to spread about the teaching. "The Church's magisterium [teaching authority] does not present truths that are impossible to live out."

This last sentence contradicts the widely-held view that, whereas mankind has lived well enough without artificial contraception since the beginning of history, this is quite impossible from the 20th century onwards. This writer has cared for thousands of good married couples who have lived happy lives according to the principles outlined by the Popes.

Ethical implications

Despite its current popularity and its being considered the norm for both married and unmarried couples, artificial contraception remains a serious moral fault, at least for those who see the issues clearly. Others will have a diminished culpability, due to their lack of perception.

This excuse can hardly be claimed by doctors, nurses and FPA staff. Their main problems stem from the matter of cooperation (see Chapter 2), which is usually indirect, proximate and either formal or material.

A special ethical problem is presented by organizations such as the Brook Clinics in England (which were set up specifically to provide contraception for minors) and by the FPA clinics which offer a service which facilitates juvenile sexual adventures.

Many governments have allowed themselves to be conned into permitting these anti-family organizations to prescribe contraceptives for children under the age of 16 (and to anesthetize and abort them) without the knowledge or permission of their parents. There could be no clearer example of the subverting of parental rights and authority, and the medical profession must accept some of the responsibility for allowing and even promoting this injustice.

Protestant theologians

A common view is that it is only Catholics who reject birth control and other sexual deviations, but in an interesting book[4] Charles Provan quotes the rejection of these common sins by 98 Protestant divines from the 16th to the 20th centuries. These include several quotes from Martin Luther (d. 1546) and John Calvin (d. 1564). Most of the discussion centers around the sin of Onan (Genesis 38:3-10) and the exegesis of this event.

CHAPTER 9

STERILIZATION

Definition

Sterilization refers to any technique that renders the subject sterile even though sexual intercourse is carried through normally. It can be temporary or permanent, medical or surgical, direct or indirect. Obviously there is some overlap with contraception, especially in the case of OCs (hormones) which create a temporary medical sterilization, but mostly we think of it as a surgical procedure which aims to produce a permanent inability to conceive.

Techniques

It is useful for a start to eliminate *indirect* sterilization because it involves no ethical problems. If, for example, a hysterectomy is performed for some legitimate reason such as heavy periods or fibroids, it certainly sterilizes the woman but this is incidental and indirect. The main aim of the operation is to treat the primary pathology. The sterility which it causes is foreseen and permitted but not directly sought, even if in some cases the patient perceives it as a bonus!

On the other hand, it is not uncommon now for patients to have hysterectomies solely for sterilizing purposes, the rationale being that this major operation is now fairly safe, it obviates future malignancy, and it saves the patient from putting up with menstruation from a now "useless" (sterile) organ. This procedure is, of course, an example of direct sterilization.

Removal of the gonads (ovaries or testicles) for malignancy renders the patient sterile, but this is an indirect effect and therefore licit. Sometimes the normal gonads are removed because they are contributing a hormone stimulus to the growth of a tumor in another organ — the testicles in cancer of the prostate or the ovaries in cancer of the breast. Both of these operations are considered justifiable despite the sterility which they cause indirectly.

But removal of normal gonads in those who simply wish for a "sex change" operation, which is mainly a psychological problem, could not be justified. The words used are actually a misnomer; the sex is not changed, it is only obscured.

Direct sterilization means in the great majority of cases the surgical destruction of the Fallopian tubes in the woman, and of the vas in the male. The tubes are essential for the passage downwards of the ovum and for the progression upwards of the sperm cells. If they are divided (tubal ligation), or banded, or removed (salpingectomy), or destroyed by diathermy or laser, the germ cells cannot encounter each other and therefore conception is impossible. In the male the vasa conduct the sperms up from the testicles to be stored in the seminal vesicle and if they are divided (vasectomy) the semen ejaculated contains no germ cells. Vasectomy is not etymologically correct, but it is entrenched in the language. A more accurate description would be "vas division and ligation" but that is too cumbersome.

Clinical implications

These apparently simple operations sometimes have a major unanticipated impact on the individuals, on society and on the national life. With such vast numbers being performed each year it is estimated (but on necessarily uncertain information) that between one quarter and one half of all young marriages in the United States are now permanently sterile. When the inevitable demographic collapse does hit the nation it will be impossible for the population dearth to be reversed. Only immigration will keep the country and its industry viable.

Many people are unaware that sterilizing operations can fail in at least one percent of cases, and up to seven percent in the worst group, as detailed in my book *The Doctor and Christian Marriage*. This is a tribute to the tendency of any hollow organ to recanalize, whether it is a tube, or a vas, or a varicose vein, or repaired hernia. Some of the failures (pregnancies) turn out to be ectopics, and for the occasional unlucky woman it may prove to be a fatal complication.

Another puzzling complication of tubal ligation is subsequent menorrhagia (heavy periods). This is by the nature of the complaint a difficult statement to prove, but many doctors and patients are convinced of its validity. Those with a simple trust in modern medicine cannot imagine that such simple operations could possibly have any remote complications, but it is still a good policy in medicine never to interfere with the normal functioning of the body. There is a strong suspicion, which may take years to confirm, that vasectomy may be associated with later urolithiasis (kidney stones) or cancer of the prostate. The latter association seems to have been demonstrated by two articles and an accompanying editorial in the *Journal of the American Medical Association*.[1,2]

Repeat Caesarean section

This subsection deserves special elucidation because it is now almost routine to sterilize the patient at the time of a second Caesarean, a decision that is more sentimental than strictly obstetrical. The concern is that in a future pregnancy the scar in the uterus may be weak and rupture during labor or at the end of her nine months gestation.

Part of the problem stems from the unquestioned American motto; "Once a Caesarean, always a Caesarean." Many hospitals have an admirable record of safety in doing repeat (second) Caesareans, but this policy has the effect of limiting family size to two children. And moreover, however safe Caesareans may be, vaginal deliver is usually safer. The policy in British countries has been to allow vaginal delivery if the indication for the original Caesarean was a non-recurring one (fetal distress, a bleeding problem, etc.).

As most young American obstetricians have never seen this policy applied nor have managed cases having multiple Caesareans, it is necessary to go to older writers to demonstrate the safety of following a conservative plan. As detailed in *The Doctor and Christian Marriage*, the *JAMA* of 1956 carried a unique article reporting patients who have had between four and ten Caesareans. I myself have done two sixth Caesareans, but in each of these cases the uterine scars were too weak to repair and therefore a hysterectomy was performed at the delivery. To some this appears heavy-handed and they ask, "Why not simply tie the tubes?" Apart from the ethical considerations, this simple management may have its own disadvantages — subsequent failure (pregnancy); or ectopic; or menorrhagia leading to hysterectomy; or later cancer of the endometrium. The decision is therefore more complicated than it appears at first sight.

Management blunders

One aspect of the sterilization explosion which is never adverted to in articles on this subject is what I call "management blunders." This refers to the often overlooked fact that fertility and childbearing are factors not just of one spouse but of both simultaneously; therefore the whole marital scene should be considered before the fateful sterilizing operation. It is not uncommon to come across cases in which one partner has had the operation without the knowledge or consent of the other. But even more tragic are those in which the husband has a vasectomy and shortly afterwards the wife has to have a hysterectomy.

Case Report

A patient came to me with vague symptoms and I discovered huge fibroids in the uterus. They had obviously been growing silently for some years. She had to have a hysterectomy — and then the fact emerged that her husband had undergone a vasectomy only three months before! His operation was not only immoral but a waste of time and money. In the privacy of the home there were probably bitter recriminations. The shortest interval I have heard of in this "blunder" drama is one month.

In an unrelated case, I once had a patient who requested a reversal of her tubal ligation. The operation had been performed only two weeks before!

Ethical assessment

Destroying the anatomy and function of normal tubes or vasa is a mutilation and therefore wrong in its very essence. It is forbidden by the Commandment, "Thou shalt not kill." This has always been understood as forbidding not only homicide but also every other act of violence against the body — suicide, torture, mutilation, wounding, careless risk to one's own health (through the abuse of alcohol, drugs, etc.) as well as carelessly putting others at risk (through drunken driving, etc.).

Many modern physicians and patients may not realize that tubal ligations and vasectomies come under the category of mutilations. But one suspects that sometimes there might be feelings of sadness that the door has been closed to them on childbearing as a result of such operations.

Case Report

I remember one woman who was having her second Caesarean for a problem of diabetes in pregnancy. Diabetes is always a tricky problem in these circumstances because the insulin requirements change rapidly and, even though the modern results are generally very good, the child is always at risk during pregnancy and immediately after delivery.

I was in the adjacent operating room when the professor did her Caesarean and sterilized her in a routine fashion. The child failed to breathe, and before the operation was over it was dead. The gift of fertility had also been lost forever. The only thing I could do was to baptize the still warm baby.

The real nature of sterilization is seen more clearly when it is removed from the area of Western culture and observed in a simpler scene. In 1977 Mrs. Indira Gandhi embarked on forced sterilization of India's poor and, instead of welcoming this relief of their impoverishment, the peasants attacked the soldiers with sticks and stones, the only weapons that they had. Her irrational policy was one of the factors which contributed to her political defeat soon afterwards.

In the 1930's Hitler launched a policy of sterilizing mentally defective persons, Gypsies and Jews, in obvious contempt for these persecuted minorities. It was a great crime against humanity which cries to heaven yet. Some American States permit punitive sterilization for some penal offences, and this raises some very serious ethical questions about the morality, the wisdom and even the usefulness of such a policy.

Cooperation

The culpability of the doctors, nurses and patients involved can be assessed according to the principles outlined in Chapter 2. But it must be admitted that for most of them, ignorant of the ethical principles involved, their culpability is probably minimal or absent. For those who do understand them, the prohibition of sterilization is absolute and no circumstances can justify its use. There are millions of couples who have not been sterilized, and for them life does not seem to be too intolerable.

Papal statements

In *Casti Connubii* (1930) Pope Pius XI condemned sterilization. In 1940, after the Nazis had launched their mass sterilization campaign, the Holy Office was asked: "Is direct sterilization of the man or the woman, permanent or temporary, lawful?" and it replied: "No, it is forbidden by the law of nature."

Pope Pius XII in his Address to Italian Midwives (1951) stated: "Direct sterilization, that is, that which seeks as a means or an end to render procreation impossible, is a serious violation of the moral law."

In his historic and controversial encyclical, *Humanae Vitae* (1968), Pope Paul VI declared: "Equally to be excluded, as the teaching authority of the Church has frequently declared, is direct sterilization, whether permanent or temporary, whether of the man or of the woman."

(The reference to "temporary" refers mainly to hormonal contraceptives which create a reversible sterility.)

CHAPTER 10

ABORTION — THE GREAT INJUSTICE

A modern holocaust

Induced abortion is one of the most incredible phenomena of the past 30 years but, our sensibilities blunted by the all-pervading violence in modern society, we are inclined to slip into an attitude of impotent acceptance. Each year throughout the world there are probably 50 million abortions. Considered solely as a loss of human lives, legalized abortion makes Hiroshima and Nagasaki, conventional warfare, and the road toll all seem like petty annoyances.

The morality of abortion

Here we need not discuss in detail the operative techniques, the present and future demographic repercussions, and the health risks of abortion. We shall limit ourselves mainly to the moral assessment.

One difficulty lies with defining the beginning of human life. Up until the 1960's it was universally accepted, as every student of embryology used to be able to tell you, that life began at conception. It is then that the chromosomal endowment from each parent united and a new unique individual started life. From that time on, he experienced only growth and development. On every passing day, he was a perfect human being with an anatomy and physiology appropriate to that stage of development. Fertilized ovum, morula, blastocyst, embryo, fetus, child — these are merely convenient labels to place on the human being as he grows. At the start of life he received his nutrition through body fluids; later through the placenta; and after birth through the digestive tract, with oxygenation coming through respiration instead of via the cord blood.

For confirmation we can turn not to a physician, to whom these things should be unquestionable, but to an educated layman (!), Pope John Paul II, who made a passing reference to this matter in a statement on abortion:[1]

> The right to life does not depend on a particular religious conviction. It is a primary, natural, inalienable right that springs from the very dignity of every human being. The defence of life *from the moment of conception* until natural death is a defence of the human person in the dignity that is his from the sole fact of existence, independently of whether that existence was planned or welcomed by the persons who gave rise to it. Every reflection on this serious matter must begin from the clear premise that procured abortion is the taking of the life of *an already existing human being.*

What erroneous statements do we now hear from modern medical graduates? That life begins not at fertilization but at implantation! This, of course, is to justify the use of IUDs and other contraceptives which act as early abortifacients. That "personhood" is gradually bestowed on the child during intrauterine life and early childhood. Personhood, an ill-favored neologism, is never defined. It gives the impression that the right to life, which up to now has always been acknowledged as the natural heritage of all human beings, born or unborn, must now be earned by proof of normality and cannot be claimed as inalienable simply by being a member of our species. No, this fundamental right is now given to the child by the physician or by the parents when they decide on an arbitrary basis which of the offspring is fit to live.

The following is an excerpt from a committee report to the Annual Meeting of the American Medical Association in Louisville, Kentucky:

> ... this body, representing as it does the physicians of the land, publicly expresses its abhorrence of the unnatural and now rapidly increasing crime of abortion; it avows its true nature as no simple offense against public morality and decency, no mere misdemeanor, no attempt upon the life of the mother, but the wanton and murderous destruction of her child.

The date of the Meeting was May, 1859 (sic). *Tempora mutantur* (How times change)! Now more than 1 1/2 million abortions are induced in the United States each year, not by criminals but by the members of the A.M.A. And the story is the same in every formerly "civilized" country.

Abortion techniques

It is not necessary to describe here the usual cruel and barbaric procedures of abortion, but the *latest* technique should be publicized because it is brilliantly clever and cold-blooded. It is "selective reduction of fetuses," which means killing off some and allowing others to survive. The problem arises in *in vitro* fertilization (IVF) where the doctor often produces multiple pregnancies with two, three or up to seven fetuses. If the pregnancies are left undisturbed, there is a high risk that the patient will deliver prematurely and this results in some stillbirths or tiny babies who might be brain-damaged with the prospect of perhaps three months of pediatric care with its attendant expense.

So the idea arose of destroying a few of the fetuses so as to improve the prognosis for their remaining brothers and sisters. As Dr. Berkowitz and colleagues reported,[2] their technique is ". . . an attempt to increase their chances of delivering infants mature enough to survive." They managed 12 such pregnancies, in which 2 patients had 6 fetuses, 1 had 5, 5 had 4, and 4 had 3. That is a total of 49 young human beings. These were "reduced" to 25 (11 patients had 2 babies, one had 3), which means that 24 were sacrificed.

How is this done? Under scan control, a "20-gauge needle was placed directly into the fetal heart[!] . . . [After the injection of potassium chloride] the heart was monitored visually [by scan] for asystole." In other words, it was watched until it stopped beating.

The justification for this rapier-like quietus was: "The financial [!] and emotional strains caused by having to raise three or more siblings simultaneously can be devastating. . . ."

It must be remembered that all these patients went into the IVF treatment freely and with full knowledge of the implications. In fact, one of the patients went through the "reduction" procedure twice.

Rape and incest

Forced intercourse and unwelcome pregnancy are the most distressing problems to handle, especially if it has been multiple incest (with several daughters) or multiple (gang) rape. The revolting injustice seems to justify any "remedy." Most governments which try to control legal abortion still make a permissive exception for cases of rape, or incest, or fetal abnormality, besides the standard excuse of "a threat to the mother's physical or mental health."

But the remedy offered is simply the killing of the resulting child by abortion. The child should not lose its right to life simply because of its objectionable origins. The injustice of the situation is only compounded if homicide (abortion) is added to it. It is not the child who should pay the penalty for the crime. This may seem a "hard saying" in the emotionally charged atmosphere engendered by these cases where the woman feels that she is being forced to pay the penalty for someone else's crime. But avoidance of abortion is the only Christian course of action permitted by the requirements of morality and justice.

Case Report

In the last case of incest at which I was obliged to appear in Court as an expert witness, the facts had not emerged until the baby was six months old. Abortion advocates would maintain that a child of rape or incest has no right to life. If they were consistent, they should have demanded that the child be killed even at the age of six months. They deplore, and quite correctly, the long purgatory of the pregnancy, the labor and delivery, and the upbringing of a child of rape or incest. Abortion is seen as a quick way of dealing with such a messy situation and assuaging the patient's distress.

Laudable as these aims may be, however, they are misguided. The psychological wounds have already been inflicted, and only time will heal them. In the case just cited the girl, aged 16, was quite self-possessed during pregnancy and delivery; the baby was adopted; the father was sentenced to jail. The girl later married and I delivered her on two later occasions. She showed no signs of any adverse effect from her ordeal. At least she had given life to the child for which she could legitimately take great pride. An abortion would have haunted her conscience for the rest of her life. The resilience of human beings enables them to recover from these stresses, just as they do from other tragedies in life, including the brutalities of war.

Emergency management

What to do if a woman seeks help immediately after a rape? Most police doctors seem either to administer the "morning after pill" or to insert an IUD. These act as abortifacients and therefore may not logically be used.

As this is not marital intercourse, the semen is present within the vagina illicitly and may be removed by the most appropriate means. Simple douching may not be sufficient because the invasion of the sperms into the cervical mucus occurs very quickly. Therefore a suction curettage of the contents of the cervical canal and uterine cavity to remove the sperm cells would be licit. If at the same time the endometrium lining of the uterus was lost, that would be an unavoidable effect. At this stage of the clinical drama, no pregnancy would be in existence.

Referral problems

How can the family doctor cope with the not uncommon legislation which obliges him to refer any patient seeking abortion to the local "termination" clinic? Legislation which forces him unwilling to cooperate in this way is unjust and no culpability would attach to the doctor.

He could assure that patient that he would give her a referring letter to the abortion clinic, and it would read as follows:

> "Dear Sir, Miss Smith wishes to attend your clinic. In my opinion there is no medical reason to justify abortion in this case. To perform one would be a repudiation of our Hippocratic Oath and a dereliction of our duty to care for our patients, both born and unborn.
> "If she should suffer any of the common complications of abortion such as hemorrhage, pelvic infection, retained products of conception, sterility, perforation of the uterus, etc., I have assured her I shall be willing to support her in any subsequent claim for damages."

It can be asserted with absolute certainty that there are no longer any medical indications to justify induced abortion. Even if the patient has a serious problem, she faces greater danger from the anesthetic and abortion operation than she does from conservative management. I have offered a $1,000 prize to anyone who can dispute this claim and so far no one has accepted the challenge.

Some years ago I wrote an article which showed, with the support of 63 references from the world literature, that "therapeutic" abortion is an untenable concept in the modern world. If my claim was true then (1968) it is doubly true now.[3]

The fetus is our patient

The family doctor who greets every new pregnant patient with the question: "Do you want it? Or do you want an abortion?" must accept some personal share in the global guilt over abortion. His approach takes advantage of a patient at a time when she is very likely nauseated, depressed, possibly unmarried, and has ambivalent feelings about having a baby. This is a time when she needs sympathy, support, encouragement and genuine love. I outline how to do this in my little book on antenatal care.[4]

The common assumption that the doctor has a responsibility towards the mother but none for the child *in utero* is both illogical and erroneous. From the time the pregnant mother puts herself in his care the doctor has *two* patients, and he has an ethical duty to provide his professional services to both of them. The fact that one of them is smaller, invisible (except on a scan) and silent does not excuse any repudiation of his ordinary medical duty.

There is no doubt that many practitioners close their minds to the facts of embryology and cannot believe that this small, even microscopic, intrauterine passenger really is a genuine human being. The IVF practitioners know he is; they even photograph him in the cellular stage and the proud parents hang the photograph on the wall at home.

Even if the mother rejects the child and asks for its elimination

through abortion, the doctor may never abandon it. He is its last line
of defence. If he ignores the call of justice and through cowardice
agrees to take the child's life, all will be lost — the child, the
mother's self-respect, the reputation of the profession, the stability
of society, everything.

Ethical assessment

Induced abortion can be defined as: the direct killing of an
innocent human being.

"Direct" — the various techniques of abortion, whether medical or surgical, are all direct attacks on the unborn child. Sometimes
the child suffers indirectly during the medical or surgical management of an unrelated condition. If it dies or aborts, there is no guilt
attaching to the doctor, even if its demise was foreseen and permitted, but it was not directly sought.

"Killing" — there is no doubt that killing the child is of the
essence in abortion, despite the confusing euphemisms with which
the procedure is surrounded — "termination of pregnancy," "selective reduction of fetuses," and the like. The truth emerges when late
abortions are performed and sometimes, possibly from a miscalcu-
lation of maturity, the child is delivered alive. There are many
recorded cases in which the doctor has strangled the baby with his
bare hands, or has drowned it, or let it bleed to death, or die from
exposure and starvation. In all these cases, the common justification
for such barbarism is that there is an unwritten contract with the
patient to produce a dead baby, not a live one.

"Innocent" — despite the hatred, even fury, directed against
the child and the ruthless techniques which ensure its demise, it is
still an innocent person. It is incapable of volitional evil. It is not "a
threat" to its mother's life, even if its presence at this time is an
inconvenient nuisance.

"Human being" — this is undeniable, as explained above.
Admittedly it is small, but human rights are not determined by a
measuring tape.

Direct induced abortion is therefore a serious moral fault. Its prohibition is absolute and no circumstances can ever justify it, even if there is a genuine serious threat to life, or to health, or to freedom, or to economic security, or to social status.

The degree of culpability of all those involved in the abortion process is outlined in the principles of cooperation in Chapter 2. It is probable that the principal actor in this domestic drama, the unfortunate young mother, is not always wholly culpable of wrong doing because her knowledge of the issues is defective (in no small part due to the media and the propaganda of pro-choice [read anti-life] advocates) and her judgment has been confused by the distressing pressures applied to her by her family, boy friend or husband. In countries such as China and her vassal, Tibet, where there is forced abortion and women are coerced or dragged screaming to abortaria, there could be no element of guilt.

Statements by Popes, the Fathers, and Church Leaders

As Hippocrates (c. 400 B.C.) demonstrates, abortion has been condemned from the earliest times, but it is only in recent years that it has become such an all-pervading moral issue.

The Christian Church has consistently opposed abortion from the beginning. The *Didache* (c. 100 A.D.), which is considered the earliest statement of Christian faith and morals, states: "You shall not kill the fetus by an abortion." Athenagoras (c. 177) and Tertullian (c. 225) both describe abortion as murder. Similar statements were made by St. Cyprian (d. 258) and St. Hippolytus (d. 235) and also by the Council of Elvira (c. 300).

St. Basil the Great (d. 375) stated: "A woman who deliberately destroys a fetus is answerable for murder. And any fine distinction as to its being completely formed or unformed is not admissible among us." In the 5th century, St. John Chrysostom, St. Augustine and St. Jerome all held similar views.

In the modern world, abortion has been condemned repeatedly in papal encyclicals and allocutions and in a reply from the Holy Office.

In *Humanae Vitae* (1968), Pope Paul VI stated (N. 14): "We must once again declare that . . . directly willed and procured abortion, even if for therapeutic reasons, [is] to be absolutely excluded as [a] licit means of regulating birth."

This constant teaching was confirmed by the Second Vatican Council (1962-1965) in *Gaudium et Spes* (The Pastoral Constitution on the Church in the Modern World). In N. 27 it states: "Furthermore, whatever is opposed to life itself, such as any type of murder, genocide, abortion, euthanasia, suicide . . . all these things and others of their like are infamies indeed."

Again in N. 51: "Therefore from the moment of its conception life must be guarded with the greatest care, while abortion and infanticide are unspeakable crimes."

Many have the impression that it is mainly, or only, the Catholic Church that opposes abortion, but that is not true. Many Protestant churches have joined and are even leading the fight against this injustice, but it must be admitted that in recent years others have suffered from an attack of cold feet or have been seduced by the arguments of the abortionists.

Dietrich Bonhoeffer, the great Lutheran theologian who was murdered by the Nazis in 1945, wrote in his *Ethics*:

"Destruction of the embryo in the mother's womb is a violation of the right to life which God bestowed upon nascent life. To raise the question whether we are here concerned with a human being or not is merely to confuse the issue. The simple fact is that God certainly intended to create a human being and that this nascent human being has been deliberately deprived of his life. And that is nothing but murder."

Two other Protestant professors expressed similar views. Helmuth Thielecke, of the University of Hamburg, said: "(O)nce conception has taken place it is no longer a question of whether the persons concerned have responsibility for a *possible* parenthood;

they have *already become* parents." Karl Barth (d. 1968), of Basle, Switzerland, said: "He who destroys germinating life kills a man."

An Orthodox Jewish statement comes from Dr. Immanuel Jakobovits, the Chief Rabbi in Britain: "Based on these principles, present-day rabbis are unanimous in condemning abortion, feticide, or infanticide to eliminate a crippled being, before or after birth, as an unconscionable attack on the sanctity of life."

Sad to say, the abortion incidence in Israel itself is one of the highest in the world and, as a consequence, the birth rate is very low. This cannot continue indefinitely. It is unthinkable that the Chosen People after all these millennia could commit race suicide and disappear. Something will have to be done to stop the destruction, not only in the Jewish state but in our own countries as well.

CHAPTER 11

HOMOSEXUALITY

Homosexuality in history

At present, homosexuality is enjoying one of its historical periodic surges of popularity. I was in boarding institutions for the whole of my primary, secondary and tertiary education; and I was in the Navy for three years, sometimes packed into the hull of a cruiser with 850 others. In all these situations I am sure that homosexuality was very rare. Now it is to be found everywhere. A great wave of hedonism has swept round the world engulfing every society. And homosexuality is one of its many expressions.

This vice is not new. There are numerous records of homosexuality in pre-Christian times. Sappho, the Greek poetess, lived on the island of Lesbos around 600 B.C. and has bestowed her own name and that of her island on female homosexuality. Aristotle (d. 323 B.C.), writing on "morbid or perverse pleasures," remarked: "(A)nd there are other morbid states that are the result of habit, like pulling out hairs and nail-biting, or eating coal and earth, and male homosexuality; because, although these come naturally to some people, others acquire them from habit, e.g. those who have been victimized since childhood."[1]

In our day he would not be popular for describing homosexuals as "morbid" or "perverse," but he had the clinical insight to

realize, long before modern psychiatry, that some of these conditions are natural "orientations" while others are associated with
damaging childhood experiences.

Plus ca change, plus la meme chose (The more things change,
the more they remain the same). Man's inventive genius has not
extended the historic range of sexual options — we are still left with
the same old deviations from normal sexual intercourse: sodomy,
fellatio, cunnilingus, sapphism, tribadism, and so forth. But what is
new is the attempts of theologians and psychiatrists to present these
activities as "normal." Many Western countries have moved to
decriminalize homosexuality, the recurring argument being that the
state or society has no juridical interest in what is done by "consent-
ing adults in private." In actual fact, what is done in the privacy of
the bedroom soon spills out to affect the whole of society; and the
burden of caring for chronic AIDS sufferers until they die is likely
to bankrupt many a public health service. Ordinary people are
frightened by the disease risk and the latent violence that accom-
pany abnormal sexual practices.

Ethical assessment

It is important to distinguish between homosexual orientation
and homosexual acts. A very small number of men and women are
born with anatomical abnormalities (intersexes, hermaphrodites,
etc.) or psychological abnormalities which direct their sexual
interest towards those of the same sex. In these tendencies they may
have diminished or absent culpability.

For the great majority of active homosexuals, however, their
esoteric practices are freely chosen. No one is forced to undertake
any specific form of sexual activity. Some psychiatrists claim that
it is "impossible" for established homosexuals to have relations
with those of the opposite sex. It may be more accurate to say that,
once they have become "hooked" on this form of sex, they have an
aversion to heterosexual acts. Doubts are cast on the exclusive

theory of homosexuality by the observation that many of those in this subculture are actually bisexual.

When a few years ago the American College of Psychiatrists were pressured to delete "homosexuality" from their traditional list of psychiatric illnesses, there was great rejoicing among homosexuals — this, they said, proved that they were "normal."

What human actions are "normal" or "right"? Human actions are normal which conform to physiological law, and right if they are in accord with moral law. No one questions, from even an elementary consideration of the anatomy and physiology of the genital organs, that they are designed for heterosexual intercourse and reproduction. The fact that bizarre use of these organs is possible does not make such sexual acts normal or right; if it did, such gross acts as bestiality would have a claim to normality since they are the expression of that person's "orientation." The confusion in the minds of legislators and of society has presented us with such anomalies as homosexual marriages performed by homosexual clergy. It is little wonder that the young, when presented with open displays of affection usually reserved to married men and women, are confused and suffer from an identity crisis.

The Old Testament references which confirm the ancient condemnation of sodomy are Genesis 18:16-33 and 19:1-29. The matter seems quite explicit and clear. The vice of sodomy, in fact, derives its name from the city of Sodom and from this biblical passage. This term has persisted through all these centuries but now there are biblical exegetes who claim that it was all a mistake, that the sin of Sodom and Gomorrah was really "lack of hospitality." The idea seems preposterous. The men of Sodom who were trying to break down Lot's door to get to his male visitors said: "Bring them out to minister to our lust." And, as further evidence that their interest was mainly sexual, not social, Lot offered his daughters as replacements. If it were not for the epic nature of the story, Lot's gesture would have seemed unbelievable; but there is no doubt that sodomy was the vice they were seeking. And mainly for this sin, the two cities of Sodom and Gomorrah were wiped off the face of the earth.

In the New Testament the condemnation of homosexuality is based on St. Paul: "And so God handed them over to the impure desires of their hearts, which led them to degrade their bodies with one another. They exchanged the truth of God for falsehood, they worshipped and paid reverence to creatures instead of to the Creator, Who is blessed forever, Amen. This is why God handed them over to dishonorable passions; indeed, even their women exchanged natural relations for those which are against nature, and similarly their men also forsook natural relations with women and burned with desire for one another — men committed shameful deeds with other men, and received a fitting punishment in their own persons for their perversion" (Romans 1:24-27).

It is not known what this last punishment was, but it may very well have involved health penalties similar to those which generally afflict those who abuse the use of sex — syphilis, gonorrhea and other sexually transmitted diseases, hepatitis, and early death. Now, of course, we have the added scourge of AIDS.

Our Lord Himself referred to the awesome penalty visited on Sodom and Gomorrah and threatened a worse fate for any city that rejected His disciples or His message: "And whoever doesn't receive you or hear your words, when you've gone out of the house or that city, shake the dust from your feet. Amen, I say to you, it will be more tolerable for the land of Sodom and Gomorrah on the day of judgment than for that city!" (Matthew 10:14-15).

In our own time, the confusion created by the sexual revolution and by dissenting theologians led the Pope to issue a clear instruction for the guidance of the faithful. In the 1975 *Vatican Declaration on Sexual Ethics*, masturbation, fornication and homosexual acts were explicitly condemned. They are wrong in all circumstances; nothing can justify them. This appears to place a heavy burden on those involved in practices of this kind, but it is not impossible to return to a normal chaste life with the help of prayer and the Sacraments of Reconciliation and the Eucharist.

Medical implications

Homosexuality presents a lot of problems to the medical profession. Physicians should not give the impression through their professional associations that homosexuality is "normal," and therefore an acceptable and morally neutral way of life which may be a sort of therapy for sexual inadequacy, or as a variation to be experimented with in marriage, or as an appropriate social union which should be given acceptance equal to that of normal hetero-sexual unions. Especially they should not assent to such partners adopting children.

This does not mean that homosexuals should be rejected or treated with less than our customary charity. They are often suffer-ing individuals, many of them psychologically disturbed, some even suicidal. The fact that many of their problems may be self-induced does not excuse us from our duty to care for them.

If they develop AIDS or ARC (AIDS related condition), they are in danger of becoming modern-day lepers, outcasts of society, our genuinely afflicted brothers. St. Paul's prediction, "the wages of sin is death" (Romans 6:23) is patently true of many offences such as murder, suicide, anger, envy, and gluttony — but if one applies it to sexual sins, there is always a storm of protest. But AIDS, as the whole world knows or should know by now, invariably and inevi-tably does lead to an early and terrible death.

In many countries the homosexual group has great political power. It often receives large sums of taxpayer's money, and it tries to promote "safe sex." Gay rights advocates and the Planned Parenthood Association have joined hands on this issue, the one to save the lives and the lifestyle of their members and the other, for racial as well as for other reasons, to limit the number of babies for which society will inevitably be held economically responsible. Ethically speaking, it is a fatally flawed agenda. Unwanted preg-nancy and AIDS are not a problem in the loving and monogamous relationship of marriage where the dignity of the couple is fostered by respect and self-control.

Feeble attempts are being made by society to control the AIDS epidemic by relying on the magical talisman, the condom, but the latex has "voids" about 5 microns in size. The condom, as everyone knows, seldom stopped pregnancy, which is a possibility on only one day of the month. If pregnancy is caused by a sperm which is about 50 microns in size, how can the condom hold back a virus of 0.1 micron in size and which is a threat every day of the month? It must be made clear that there is absolutely no proof that condom usage reduces the incidence of HIV infection or AIDS. Nor could there be. The disease has been recognized only since 1980 and, since it has a latency period of 7 to 10 years before a clinical diagnosis can be made, it is still too early to know what effect condom use is or is not having. Other safe sex recommendations are vulgar, even unprintable.

In every other comparable threat to personal health, doctors advise patients to abstain from the noxious factors which cause disease — to give up alcohol, or smoking, or eating too much, or (sometimes) jogging. But there seems to be an unwritten rule that one must never ask homosexuals to give up sodomy or oral sex. Yet that is their only hope of avoiding AIDS.

Note that the reason why Church leaders oppose the handing out of condoms to the young as part of any so-called safe sex campaign is different from their opposition to condom use by heterosexual couples. In the latter (see Chapter 8) there is the element of nullifying fertility and also the artificial alteration of the nature of the male organ. The Ten Commandments prohibit fornication in deed or desire and, hence, any sexual activity outside of marriage. Such acts, with or without the use of birth control devices, are always wrong. In homosexual activity, of course, there is no question of any influence on fertility. And if sodomy is performed, it makes little difference if a prophylactic device is used or not. The action is equally sinful in either circumstance.

The risk to the young of presenting condom distribution as an official policy, especially at schools, is that it will encourage both homosexual and heterosexual experimentation, and it will give the impression that most adults are indifferent to such activities whereas most parents are demonstrably against them. The Medical Association should not be giving its assent to such hazardous and futile projects. You'll notice that you don't hear anything about mounting a campaign to hand out clean needles in schools for the purpose of "preventing the spread of AIDS."

Another of the kid-glove approaches to homosexuality is that every serious infectious disease in most countries is notifiable to the Department of Health, with the sole exception of AIDS. The reason given is that such a policy will encourage the patients to come in for treatment instead of hiding out from the authorities. The same argument could of course be applied to every infectious disease, and should logically lead to the dismantling of the whole system.

Confidentiality is a major dilemma. If the patient is HIV positive he will ultimately develop AIDS, but in the meantime he is a risk to his male or female partners. If he does not stop having sex with them, they will all eventually die. What should the doctor do? Does his duty of confidentiality prevent him from warning others of their life risks? The duty, of course, lies first with the infected patient, but if — as is not uncommon — he refuses to pass on the warning it seems only a temporizing measure to discuss the matter with the local medical authorities. Someone soon has to make a definite move to protect others.

It can be reasonably argued that the duty of confidentiality is not absolute when not only the health but the lives of others are being placed at risk. The patient who is taking such a reckless and unloving approach to the welfare of those closest to him loses his claim to autonomy and confidentiality. The doctor it would seem, would be justified in taking the initiative in these cases, and passing on the warning, even if this might impact negatively on the relationships involved.

Doctors and nurses at risk

AIDS, of course, can be transmitted by other than sexual means. The use of infected needles has long been known to be one source. Transfusions of infected blood is another. Babies born of an infected mother often acquire the disease in the womb.

Dr. T.W. O'Connor described the elaborate and expensive precautions which must be taken in the Operating Room when an AIDS patient is on the table.[2] These possibly unnecessary procedures are forced on them when a patient refuses to have an HIV blood test before an operation. In the San Francisco General Hospital, 33 percent of all surgical patients are HIV positive. The risk is greatest for orthopedic surgeons, because their high-speed bone saws and drills produce a spray of blood and bone particles. They, therefore, operate in something like a space suit to protect themselves. Nurses must be especially careful in the way they handle needles and other surgical instruments which have come into contact with possibly infected blood. Obstetricians and gynecologists are well-advised to take special precautions in their examinations and at the time of the child's birth when the mother is known or thought to be infected. Dentists are likewise at risk when bleeding occurs in the course of their treatment of HIV positive patients. The sterilization of instruments in all these cases must be done with extreme care before being used on other patients.

Doctors, of course, must accept any urgent cases that present themselves, but in non-urgent conditions the question arises as to why they should risk their lives to serve patients who refuse to have a diagnostic blood test before surgery. Surgeons would be justified in not performing non-urgent procedures (varicose veins, hernias, piles, etc.) in such cases.

The whole matter has been dominated by those in the news media, in politics, entertainment, in the human rights movement and the sexual revolution, but in the end, as O'Connor points out: "AIDS must be seen for what it is — another infectious (viral) epidemic which should be treated as any other disease which has afflicted mankind in the past, such as tuberculosis, leprosy, syphilis and the plague."

CHAPTER 12

FERTILITY, STERILITY, IVF, ARTIFICIAL INSEMINATION

A modern paradox

It may seem an anomaly that the gynecologist, through contraception, sterilization and abortion, helps large numbers of patients to abolish their fertility and then tries in various ways to boost the fertility of those who bemoan their inability to have children. But this may be quite proper, providing he uses only licit procedures — and there are very few of these available in this field.

Male fertility

The main ethical problems arise in the investigation of male fertility through examination of the semen. This is usually accomplished by requesting a specimen of semen. As masturbation, which is the usual method of obtaining this specimen, is wrong in all circumstances and, as the end does not justify the means, this technique may never be used. Surely there must be some other way. Is this the extent of medical ingenuity?

As there is virtually no treatment if any defect is discovered in males (and only a few cases who can be helped among the females), the patients should realize that the principal, if not the whole, thrust of sterility work is diagnostic, not therapeutic. Its importance is to sort out couples into three groups: those who appear to be normal (these should wait patiently for conception and not rush into doubtful operative procedures); men with low sperm counts (oligospermia); and those with complete absence of sperms (azoospermia). Those in these latter two groups should be encouraged to adopt a child.

The necessary diagnosis can be made fairly well, but not with absolute precision, by the traditional Sims (or Huhner) test in which the cervical mucus is examined for sperms after normal intercourse. But a better method is the examination of the semen that drains away from the male urethra after the end of the normal act. This is only a small amount, but it is sufficient for diagnostic purposes. After all, a whole hematological diagnosis can be made by examining a single drop of blood. Something similar obviously can be done with semen.

Technique: The patient is given a glass microscope slide and a delicate coverslip to go with it, both carefully wrapped together to avoid breakage. The couple then have intercourse during laboratory hours. Immediately after withdrawal, the husband allows a few drops of semen from his urethral orifice to fall onto the slide and then applies the coverslip to it. This specimen will remain moist for 2-3 hours. It is taken without delay to the designated laboratory for microscopic examination. During transport the slide should be placed in a small box, not wrapped as before or it will dry out too quickly. The test occasionally has to be repeated, but most men appreciate the natural features of this procedure when compared to masturbation.

The specimen provides information on: the density of sperm cells (expressed in numbers); their morphology (percentages of normal and abnormal forms); and their motility (percentage which are moving actively). The common masturbation specimen provides the following additional information: volume of ejaculate; pH (acidity); viscosity (flow characteristics); liquefaction; and total count (volume x density). And many laboratories add some other esoteric observations. Note that, while the information in this latter list may be interesting, it does not add anything significant to the diagnosis of fertility, and furthermore any deviation from "normal" standards is not amenable to treatment anyway. The patient therefore loses nothing by opting for the postcoital technique.

In the postcoital specimen the density of sperm cells, which is the single most important factor to investigate, is reported as so many per high power field. In round figures a count of 100 per HPF is roughly equivalent to 100 million per ml. in the full ejaculate; 50 to 50 per HPF; 10 to 10. A complete absence of sperms makes the diagnosis of azoospermia.

I first publicized this simple and elegant test in 1959.[1] The test was then included in a standard American textbook on pathology.[2] A fuller description was given in an American journal of medical ethics.[3] It supersedes and makes unnecessary the older procedures which had been tried as alternatives to masturbation — prostatic massage, testicular biopsy or needle aspiration of the seminal vesicle. And the undignified, even silly, perforated condom. When is a condom not a condom?

In vitro fertilization (IVF)

As there are virtually no ethical issues in the investigation and treatment of infertility in women, this discussion will limit itself to IVF which is a veritable ethical minefield. When Drs. Steptoe and Edwards in 1978 delivered the first IVF baby, Louise Brown, in Oldham, England, they opened a Pandora's Box from which escaped many more problems, I am sure, than they had envisaged. Many years ago I was a fellow Registrar with Steptoe in St. Mary Islington Hospital, London. He was a handsome young chap with an agreeable manner who told me that he had once been an altarboy. Now he is dead, God rest him.

At first IVF was used for patients with tubal obstruction, but now it has proven success with many other pathologies. The full title should be IVF plus ET (embryo transfer); and now there are so many acronyms that it is difficult to keep up with them — GIFT, ZIFT, PROST, LTOT, etc., many of them associated with AID and AIH (artificial insemination by donor or by husband). There is a "donation" not only of spermatozoa but also of ova, of embryos (frozen "spare" new lives), and a leasing arrangement of uteri of surrogate mothers ("wombs for hire").

The scientific techniques involved are dazzling in their planning and complexity; and the emotional appeal of the sterile couple now holding their own beautiful baby is so overwhelming that it seems churlish to raise a voice of protest and say that the whole concept is philosophically flawed. Paradoxically it can be quite proper to welcome a new innocent life into the world, but to deplore the circumstances of its conception — which may have been rape, incest or even IVF.

Ethical assessment

The most efficient way of coping with a subject of such protean manifestations is to take brief quotations from the most authoritative ethical statement available to guide both doctors and patients. This statement is *Donum Vitae* (The Gift of Life) which was issued by Cardinal Ratzinger and Archbishop Bovone, with the explicit approval of Pope John Paul II, in 1987. Its subtitle was: "Instruction on Respect for Human Life in its Origin and on the Dignity of Procreation. Replies to Certain Questions of the Day." Its intellectual force is as admirable as its ethical clarity.

"Advances in technology have now made it possible to procreate apart from sexual relations through the meeting *in vitro* of the germ cells previously taken from the man and the woman. But what is technically possible is not for that very reason morally admissible."

"Human life is sacred because from its beginning it involves the creative action of God and it remains forever in a special relationship with the Creator, who is its sole end. God alone is the Lord of life from its beginning until its end; and no one can, in any circumstances, claim for himself the right to destroy directly an innocent human being."

"(T)he gift of human life must be actualized [achieved and accepted] in marriage through the specific and exclusive acts of husband and wife, in accordance with the laws inscribed in their persons and in their union."

"Personhood" is a neologism which has been seized on by IVF and abortion doctors because it seems to depreciate the status of the fetus and allows for their sometimes nefarious activities. The concept is that the zygote, embryo, fetus is not fully human until it has achieved personhood, whatever that means.

"From the time the ovum is fertilized a new life is begun which is neither that of the father nor of the mother; it is rather the life of a new human being with his own growth. It would never be made human if it were not already human . . . (H)ow could a human individual not be a human person?"

"(E)xperimentation on embryos which is not directly thera-peutic is illicit . . . It is immoral to produce human embryos destined to be exploited as disposable biological material [for experiments or transplantation]."

Commenting on the practice of discarding "spare" or abnor-mal embryos: "It is therefore not in conformity with the moral law deliberately to expose to death human embryos obtained *in vitro.*"

Many people have an instinctive rejection of the artificiality of IVF, but find it hard to articulate the ethical dilemma which confronts them. The authors of *Donum Vitae* clarify several difficult issues. Concerning the production of hybrids resulting from the union of human sperm with animal ova, which is surely the most degrading experiment yet devised by IVF practitioners, they said: ". . . [regarding] fertilization between human and animal gametes and the gestation of human embryos in the uteri of animals, or the hypothesis or project of constructing artificial uteri for the human embryo . . . These procedures are contrary to the *human dignity proper to the embryo*, and at the same time are contrary to the right of every person to be conceived and to be born within marriage and from marriage."

Referring to the artificial and asexual production of human beings: "Also, attempts or hypotheses for obtaining a human being without any connection with sexuality through 'twin fission', cloning or parthenogenesis are to be considered contrary to the moral law, since they are in opposition to the dignity both of human procreation and of the conjugal union."

"The freezing of embryos (cryopreservation), even when carried out in order to preserve the life of an embryo, constitutes an offence against the respect due to human beings by exposing them to grave risks of death or harm to their physical integrity and depriving them, at least temporarily, of maternal shelter and gestation, thus placing them in a situation in which further offences and manipulation are possible."

Many people are upset by the statement that the majority of IVF practitioners are also active in the abortion field, which seems at first sight to be a paradox, but there is a perfectly logical progression from the first activity to the second. In fact IVF patients must usually give explicit or implicit agreement to early amniocentesis if they become pregnant, the rationale being that they will have an abortion if any abnormality is discovered.

The authors of *Donum Vitae* remarked on this situation: "The connection between IVF and the voluntary destruction of human embryos occurs too often. This is significant — through these procedures, with apparently contrary purposes, life and death are subjected to the decision of man, who thus sets himself up as the giver of life and death by decree."

One procedure that *Donum Vitae* did not advert to is that the semen, usually from the husband but sometimes from a donor, must be obtained by masturbation and this might occur when the husband is miles away from his wife. The fault here is that the transfer of the germ cells between husband and wife must take place only within the context of the normal loving sexual embrace, as designed by the Creator. This is another fundamental ethical error of IVF.

Surrogate mothers

Sometimes a woman other than the wife will carry the baby through pregnancy and delivery, and surrender it when it is born. In some cases the new zygote is transplanted into her womb (the baby has the genetic material from its father and mother, not from the surrogate); or the surrogate is fertilized by the husband's semen (she is therefore also the genetic mother); or the ovum and sperm might come from unconnected "donors" (the baby would have no genetic inheritance from the husband or the wife or the surrogate).

On Christmas Day, 1993, a 59-year-old woman in Britain gave birth to twins. She had been impregnated by Dr. Severino Antinori, of Rome, who fertilized an ovum from a younger woman with her husband's sperm. He has done a similar service for a 61-year-old woman. Such procedures must be seen as stunts; they can be done but they ought not to be. As *Donum Vitae* points out, this is an insult to the dignity of the resulting baby. This condemnation is not made merely on esthetic or prudential grounds; such manipulation of another human being, the baby, is a moral fault.

A similar judgment must be made of the use of a white woman's ovum to enable a black mother to have a white baby. The latest horror story in this field is the suggestion from Edinburgh University that, following their successful experiments in mice, it would be possible to use the ova from aborted fetuses to make up for the shortage of "donor" eggs. Thus a child could be conceived from a "mother" (a fetus) who had never been born. The evil of abortion expands exponentially.

In 1993 a 60-year-old Italian woman was impregnated by IVF plus ET, the ovum coming from her own daughter and the sperm from her son-in-law. In a field which now produces bizarre examples, this must be the ultimate.

Donum Vitae states: "Surrogate motherhood represents an objective failure to meet the obligations of maternal love, of conjugal fidelity, and of responsible motherhood; it offends the dignity and the right of the child to be conceived, carried in the womb, brought into the world and raised by his own parents; it sets up, to the detriment of families, a division between the physical, psychological and moral elements which constitute those families."

The moral norm for sexuality

Donum Vitae continues: "The Church's teaching on marriage and human procreation affirms the *inseparable connection*, willed by God and unable to be broken by man on his own initiative, between the two meanings [essential elements] of the conjugal act, the unitive [loving] meaning and the procreative meaning [fertility]."

The only morally unexceptionable variety of IVF is where the ovum of the wife is transferred to an accessible position within the uterus and the transfer of the semen is achieved by normal loving intercourse.

The child

The main emphasis in IVF and also artificial insemination is on the woman and her desire to be fulfilled through reproduction. In the best circumstances the child is welcomed and loved, but often its status and interests are ignored, even rejected. The child becomes an object which can be bought or sold, disputed over in litigation, aborted, frozen, and his organs traded for transplantation.

Donum Vitae comments: "The child is not an object to which one has a right, nor can he be considered as an object of ownership: rather, a child is a gift, 'the supreme gift,' and the most gratuitous gift of marriage, and is a living testimony to the mutual giving [loving] of his parents."

When these issues of IVF and artificial insemination were clarified by *Donum Vitae*, the Press Association commented that "any Catholic who willingly and knowingly violated this directive would be committing sin." But the majority of patients, dazzled by the scientific advances and confused by their equally confused physicians, could probably plead ignorance. For the more enlightened, *Roma locuta est, causa finita est* (Rome has spoken, and the matter is closed).

To show that the papacy is always *au courant* with scientific advances and well aware of their long term implications, it is sufficient to quote Pope Pius XII who clearly foresaw the problems that were to burst on the scene 22 years later with the first IVF birth. Addressing the Second World Congress on Sterility (1956), he said: "On the subject of the experiments in artificial fecundation *in vitro*, let it suffice for us to observe that they must be rejected as immoral and absolutely illicit."

Artificial insemination by husband (AIH)

This is indicated in only a few cases. If there is some anatomical defect such as epispadias or hypospadias in which the ejaculate cannot be placed near the cervix, it is obviously licit to collect the semen as best one can and transfer it to the external os and the cervical canal ("assisted insemination"). The essential requirement is that the act of intercourse must be carried through normally. Regrettably the usual instruction to patients is to produce a masturbation specimen, and that is always wrong.

Another two variations on this theme have emerged in recent years. One is that, in cases of oligospermia (too few sperm cells) the semen is produced by masturbation and then is centrifuged to increase their concentration. Sometimes several ejaculates are collected on successive days and the concentrate is then introduced into the vagina. Another is to separate the male sperm cells, which carry the Y-chromosome, from the female cells, which have only the X-chromosome. This procedure is made possible because of the different sizes of the heads of the spermatozoa.

The Japanese clinics which offer this service claim about a 70 percent success rate in achieving the "right" sex. Quite apart from the masturbation issue, these procedures are illicit for the reasons given above, namely that they offend against the dignity of the child and of the sexual relationship. Moreover, fostering the idea that some children are more desirable than others, it is not surprising to find that abortions are often procured for no other reason than that the child is of the "wrong" sex. This is now common in China and India; and it has been reported in England where it was a matter of an hereditary title which could pass only to a male heir!

Artificial insemination by donor (AID)

There is a considerable overlap between AID and IVF, the same practitioners offering both services and similar ethical issues being shared by each. AID aims to remedy the situation where the husband has few or no sperm cells; Mr. Donor has more than he needs, *ergo* inject some of them into the wife. The possible permutations and combinations now make one dizzy. Sperms from Mr. Husband or Mr. Donor; ova from Mrs. Wife or Ms. Donor; embryo implanted in the womb of Mrs. Wife or Ms. Donor or Ms. Surrogate or Ms. Lesbian. And with each donor fathering large numbers of secret children, the mind boggles at the implications.

With the incidence of old-fashioned illegitimacy (now called "exnuptial" because it sounds better) now running at 33 percent in my own country, it is enough to make a genealogist weep. Or go out of business.

The Warnock Report

Because of the chaos created by doctors and lawyers in this matter, the British Government in 1984 set up a committee headed by Dame Mary Warnock to give some guidance in the matter. The main findings were as follows (my comments in parentheses):

— Research on human embryos acceptable up to day-14. (This, of course, is a gross infringement on the human rights of the embryo.)
— Trans-species (human-animal) hybrids should not be allowed to develop beyond the two-cell stage. (Producing monsters is a gross injustice and should have been prohibited absolutely.)
— The sale of gametes or embryos permitted under license. (Another injustice to the developing child.)
— Preserving the anonymity of ovum and semen donors.
— Donors in AID limited to 10 children. (In Australia, 30.)
— AID children to be regarded as the legitimate offspring of the mother and her husband. (A harmful falsehood.)
— AID donors to have no rights over their children and no duties, financial or social, towards them. (Another injustice, equivalent to a Rakes' Charter.)
— The husband to be registered as "the father" of an AID child. (Another falsehood to which doctors and lawyers ought not to give their assent.)
— In cases of ovum donation, the female giving birth to be regarded as "the mother." The donor to have no rights over the child and no obligations to it. (Another injustice.)
— Surrogate motherhood to be outlawed. (!)
— Matters of inheritance and of primogeniture were defined.
— Prohibits postmortem IVF (after the husband has died).

The whole exercise was a sad revelation of the poverty of the ethical principles held by otherwise prominent people.

Ethical assessment of artificial insemination

With the exception of "assisted" insemination by the husband, all other activities in this field are morally illicit. One reason is the invariable acceptance of masturbation as part of the standard technique. Another is the separation of the loving from the fertile aspect of intercourse. More serious in AID is the introduction of the semen, and therefore the genetic material, of a third party into the body of the wife. This offends against the exclusive nature of the marital contract, and it constitutes a technical form of adultery.

Papal statements

AID was first condemned in 1897 (sic) in a Holy Office decree that was approved by Pope Leo XIII. In his address to the International Congress of Catholic Doctors (1949), Pope Pius XII said: "With regard to artificial fecundation, not only is there reason to be extremely reserved, but it must be absolutely rejected. In speaking thus, one is not necessarily forbidding the use of certain artificial means destined solely to facilitate the natural act or to achieve the attainment of the natural act normally performed." (This refers to assisted insemination.) He pointed out that marriage rights are "exclusive, non-transferable and inalienable."

In 1958 the Archbishop of Westminster made an important statement on AID: "A man or woman who has part in such degrading practices, committing solitary sin and depriving the artificially produced child of the right to be born in lawful wedlock of husband and wife as Nature demands, grievously frustrates the plan of God."

Donum Vitae states: "Heterologous artificial fertilization (AID) is contrary to the unity of marriage, to the dignity of the spouses, to the vocation proper to parents, and to the child's right to be conceived and brought into the world in marriage and from marriage [acts] . . . Furthermore, the artificial fertilization of a woman who is unmarried [that is, single, *de facto* partners, lesbians] or a widow, whoever the donor may be, cannot be morally justified."

CHAPTER 13

PREGNANCY AND DELIVERY

Miscarriage

For most women a miscarriage, whether spontaneous (accidental) or induced (legal or criminal abortion), is a traumatic experience, often alarming, sometimes dangerous. With the common spontaneous miscarriages they may suffer torments of self-doubt. Was it my fault? Should I have seen the doctor earlier? Gone to bed for days or weeks? Should I have baptized the material that came away? The answer to these questions is almost always, No. The stage is usually set a long time before the bleeding starts; no treatment makes any difference to the outcome, least of all bed rest; most times no recognizable fetus is seen; it has been dead for a long time before it is passed, therefore baptism does not apply.

It is different in cases of induced abortion or premature delivery. In these cases, if the mother's assent can be obtained, the nurse should baptize the fetus or the dismembered body that comes to her from an abortion.

If a child or fetus has died without being baptized, it is always a consolation to the mother to remind her of the universal salvific will of God. St. Paul said: "God our Savior desires that all may be saved" (1 Timothy 2:4). In His justice He must have some mechanism for saving all those who have had no access to baptism; they would not be lost because of what seems a technicality. The question as to the fate of the unbaptized must always remain a matter of uncertainty; but the mercy of God towards His frail and suffering children is a consoling and enduring certainty. I discussed this matter in a previous article.[1]

Amniocentesis and CVS

These audacious and clever techniques, along with ultrasound scans, have ushered in the era of antenatal diagnosis of many pathologies affecting the fetus, and they have also facilitated both medical and surgical treatment of the unborn child. For the first time the child is seen as a patient, and the new science of caring for him is called "fetology."

In amniocentesis the technique is used at 16-18 weeks of pregnancy. A long needle is passed into the sac surrounding the fetus and 20 ml. of liquor (the fluid surrounding the baby) is withdrawn. The cells shed into the liquor and its chemistry enable many important diagnoses to be made.

CVS (chorionic villus sampling) is done at 8-10 weeks; a needle sucks out some of the placental tissue and this provides histological diagnoses, notably neural tube defects (spina bifida or anencephaly) or Down's syndrome (mongolism).

Late amniocentesis (after 28 weeks) is designed to plan treatment for the child if, say, it is affected by Rh sensitization. Early amniocentesis and CVS are performed in order to plan an abortion for an affected child. There is therefore a world of difference between the two projects. The first is morally neutral, while the second, as part of the abortion decision, is obviously wrong in all situations.

Not only that, there is about a 5 percent chance of accidental miscarriage after these procedures, as is explained in more detail in *The Doctor and Christian Marriage*. As the overall incidence of abnormality is only about one percent, the treatment is worse than the disease.

Many patients do not understand the implications of agreeing to these exciting new investigations. It should be spelled out to them that *there is no point*, in fact it is only foolish clinical curiosity, in having them performed unless there is a prior commitment to abortion if the laboratory report is disappointing. Besides the miscarriage risk, there have been numerous reports of needle stick injuries to the baby at this critical stage of development.

Labor and delivery

Are there any ethical problems in this area? One has cause to wonder. In the past 20 years the Caesarean incidence in the United States (and a similar trend is found in most Western countries) has risen from a national average of 5 percent to 20 percent. If that is the average figure, some hospitals must have a Caesarean rate of about 40 percent. The surgical induction rate used to be about 10 percent; now one finds rates of almost 50 percent. These figures border on the absurd. Women know that there is not that much pathology in childbearing.

Part of the explanation for these high rates is the advent of "defensive medicine" which has been caused by rapacious and aggressive lawyers; partly it is the temptation of higher fees for operative procedures. This latter decision would be quite immoral. Ideally, all obstetric patients should be charged the same standard fee, whatever the mode of delivery. The doctor has a duty to serve the best interest of the patient, even if this sometimes calls for courage and stamina.

The abnormal child

It is easy to forget that our duty in medicine is to serve the abnormal, the pathological, as much as the normal. They are all children of God, our brothers, however misshapen, repulsive or immature they may be, however short their expectation of life. They have an inalienable right to life which derives not from the legislature or from the profession but from God, and therefore their lives may not be taken arbitrarily. We must give them at least ordinary care and leave their eventual demise to natural processes.

Anencephaly

The anencephalic fetus has no bone or skin over the top of its head; the undeveloped brain is exposed; it has a hopeless prognosis and usually dies within an hour of birth. The diagnosis is usually made early by screening blood tests, amniocentesis, ultrasound scan or X-rays. It is almost routine to "get rid of it" by early induction, which is actually an abortion, but even responsible obstetricians justify this on the grounds that the child will inevitably die. There is also an unspoken atavistic rejection of the abnormal, and the gratuitous assumption that these pathetic specimens have no right to life, brief though it may be.

The only ethical management of these cases is to await the spontaneous onset of labor. This also proves to be the safest thing for the patient, but it demands of her patience and acceptance of the prospect of a dead baby. In these matters, women have a greater capacity for courage than do male obstetricians. Our duty is to lend them our strength and not to participate in the general atmosphere of hysteria surrounding them.

Hydrocephalus

It need hardly be said that there is no clinical justification, much less ethical approval, for abortion in these cases. The child has an enlarged head from excess cerebrospinal fluid within the cavities of the brain. It is a serious condition but shunt operations have improved the prognosis and many of these children are almost normal despite some thinning of the cortex. If there is an associated spina bifida, the management becomes more difficult but by no means hopeless.

Management during labor

Many cases are diagnosed only at the end of pregnancy or during labor. A Caesarean delivery is an easy choice, but it is still traumatic for the child and not necessarily preferable to vaginal delivery. By either route there is some unavoidable compression and possibly collapse of the skull, and this may prove fatal.

If tapping of the ventricles is an acceptable procedure for treatment postpartum, there is no ethical reason why this should not be done intrapartum. The ventricles can be tapped either *per abdomen* or *per vaginam* during labor. The latter is an easy procedure if the head is presenting and the cervix dilated more than 4 cm. A long needle or canula is inserted through the skin and thinned out cranial bones and the fluid drains away slowly, thus reducing the head size.

If the baby is presenting by the breech, a Caesarean is the obvious choice, but sometimes the obstetrician encounters an emergency situation where the diagnosis has not been made until late in labor. He might find the legs and trunk delivered but the head is held up above the brim of the pelvis. Once again a needle or canula can be passed through the lambdoidal suture line and the fluid allowed to escape until the head is small enough to be delivered. A high mortality is unavoidable.

One of my colleagues once told me how distressing it was in these circumstances to pass a metal catheter or similar hard instrument through the foramen magnum and destroy the brain stem while the child wriggled in protest. This was quite unnecessary. The cord was prolapsed and being pressed on at the pelvic brim. If he had waited a few minutes the baby would inevitably have died from cord pressure. Once it was dead he would then be free to employ any delivery procedure he wished without offending morality or his emotional sensitivity. While waiting for this sad ending, he could have baptized the child.

Spina bifida

Babies with a large spinal defect and sac (meningomyelocele) are not a pretty sight, but they should not be dumped on the scrap heap. Most of them now come to midtrimester abortions. The child is usually normal from the waist up; and neurosurgery can sometimes improve the associated leg paralysis. Many of these children are happy and intelligent, and they lead fulfilled lives even if confined to wheelchairs.

Screening for neural tube defects

These neural tube defects (NTD) can be screened for by checking blood specimens for alphafetoprotein (AFP). But, as with amniocentesis, there is no point in having this test unless there is a strong probability of abortion if the child is affected. To show that modern medicine is not infallible, we have seen more than one case in which abortion was performed on the basis of a positive AFP or scan report, and yet no NTD was found. The children were quite normal. This is the sort of tragic blunder from which women of good ethical standards are protected. Real mothers understand their duty to care for their children, whether perfect or imperfect, because each one is still a child of God and precious in His eyes. As He said about all human beings in the Old Testament: "You are precious in my eyes and I love you" (Isaiah 43:4).

Fortunately for parents who have had one NTD child and know that there is a tendency to recurrence of this defect in future pregnancies, there is great hope for the future, thanks to the pioneering work of Professor R.W. Smithells of Leeds, England.

The Medical Research Council (MRC) undertook a huge randomized double-blind trial of vitamin prophylaxis, involving

1817 women who had had a previous NTD child. To gather such a large number of subjects involved in a fairly rare disease, they had to seek cooperation from obstetricians and pediatricians in seven countries. They found that "72 percent of [potential] NTDs were prevented." "Our results show that *folic acid* supplementation can prevent NTDs."[2]

The other most vulnerable class in modern obstetricians' "search and destroy" missions in that of children with Down's Syndrome. Unfortunately, in many countries permissive abortion legislation purports to give patients the "right" to abort their defective offspring, and there have been cases of doctors being prosecuted for failing to arrange amniocentesis for "at risk" women. They are charged with a "wrongful life" offence, that is, they produced a live abnormal baby when, in the view of the patient and the law, they should have killed it at an early stage. Was there ever a more grotesque operation of the law?

To protect himself, the ethical obstetrician who has a patient over 37 years old or with a past history of fetal abnormality must present her with a written statement along these lines: "Some physicians would advise amniocentesis, or CVS, and so forth in cases like yours. I do not because I think it is wrong, dangerous, illogical and cruel. But if you wish to have it done, you are at liberty to consult some other obstetrician."

If she has any sense, she will realize that she will get better care from a doctor who has some ethical standards than from one who is less principled. Will a doctor who is willing to sacrifice the child in early pregnancy be reliable at the end and during labor? Which type of practitioner will be more likely to sacrifice his own convenience in order to serve the best interests of mother and baby? Which will be influenced by such irrelevant considerations as whether the baby is wanted or unwanted, legitimate or illegitimate, black or white, rich or poor?

The answer should be obvious: good medicine and good morals go hand in hand. On *a priori* grounds there could be no conflict between them, because the same Creator designed the human body and the human soul. Bad ethics, although having a certain short-term attraction, must always produce bad medicine. This is because once we abandon love and justice we also abandon truth, and the scientific method depends ultimately on the search for truth — about the patient and about society.

Postpartum and postnatal concerns

The days immediately after delivery are the times when so many women have a sterilizing operation. As explained before, this is both unwise and unethical for those who see the issues clearly.

Is there any ethical problem in deciding not to *breast-feed* the baby? There probably is — but it would be only a minor fault. It is basically a matter of depriving the newborn baby of its nutritional heritage. In recent decades, the United States has been out of step with the rest of the world in preferring formula feeding (bottle feeding, artificial feeding) to breast-feeding, but there are some signs of a change of attitude in society.

Once again, "the physiological is the optimum" — breast-feeding is obviously the design of the Creator, and clever doctors cannot improve on it. The milk is the perfect nutrition for the baby, and moreover it contains antibodies to common infections. The suckling reflex from the nipple stimulates the mother's pituitary gland which in turn causes contraction of the uterus. This cuts down the blood loss and speeds the return to normal of the pelvic organs. Moreover, the act of feeding brings an elemental satisfaction to both mother and baby.

This must be regarded as the norm; but many mothers afflicted by a poor milk supply, or by inverted or cracked nipples, have to be content with formula feeding. It is amazing how well babies thrive on this essentially second-best regimen.

At the 6-weeks postnatal check, the modern fashion is to ensure that every patient is fitted up with some form of contraception, especially if she is unmarried. Many doctors cannot comprehend that some of these women would prefer not to have this service. And, in the unmarried group, universal availability of contraception has been a complete failure as it mainly encourages more sex and inevitably more pregnancies. The common assumption that the doctor is the one who should be responsible for controlling every aspect of these women's private lives is an example of sexual paternalism, which is reminiscent of the state paternalism that is at the heart of socialism.

At St. Vincent's Hospital for unmarried mothers where I cared for some 2,000 patients over the years, we neither lectured them and certainly never gave them contraceptives when they were discharged. They were in residence for some weeks before delivery, and they gradually absorbed the unspoken message about how to behave. If they wanted to talk, I would say nothing more than: Keep away from bad company — you know the types of boys who are bad news for you. Don't drink too much. And (if they had any religious affiliation) go to church every Sunday without fail. It is impossible to follow up this type of patient, but we never had any evidence to regret our style of management of the problem.

Ectopic pregnancy

Ectopics, once a rare complication of pregnancy, are now fairly common and have become a leading cause of maternal mortality. This serious increase has been most marked since 1970 and has been attributed to several factors which now characterize the sexual practices of society, namely: the frequency of tubal sterilization; the use of IUDs; the introduction of progesterone-only OCs ("mini-pill"); and pelvic infection (salpingitis) resulting from promiscuity or induced abortion. Many of the ectopic sufferers are therefore victims of the sexual revolution. But it should be pointed out that no specific cause can be found for many ectopics. They can occur in women of the utmost rectitude.

In the operative management there is seldom any ethical problem, because the embryo or fetus is usually dead by the time they come to surgery. The damaged tube must be removed, even if this diminishes fertility, or, if the other tube has previously been removed, it causes an indirect sterilization. Sometimes gynecologists will try to conserve the tube by incising it and shelling out the pregnancy; or by milking it out of the fimbriated end of the tube. But this is sentimental surgery and not really in the patient's best interests. It leaves her with a damaged tube and, while she occasionally may have a normal pregnancy in the future, the risks of a further (third) ectopic are greatly increased.

Case Report

I once had to see an emergency case who opened the consultation by saying, "I've got an ectopic." Being your average pompous type of doctor, I felt like saying, "You tell me your symptoms, I'll tell you the diagnosis." But she was right! I could hardly believe it. The story was that she had an original ectopic; then a second one and at this operation the surgeon tried to conserve the remaining tube. Sure enough, she later had this third ectopic. For a short time her life had been in danger, thanks to the sentimental surgery on the second occasion.

The ethical dilemma occurs when an ectopic is diagnosed before tubal rupture, that is, before the fetus has died. With the use of laparoscopy and ultrasonic scans, this early diagnosis occurs more frequently. The tube will certainly rupture in the next week or two, with grave risk to the mother. The surgeon is confronted with a pathological tubal swelling and he is justified in removing it, even though the fetus will surely die. Its death is indirect; it is foreseen and permitted, but not directly willed. Admittedly this is a fine distinction in ethics, but the procedure described appears to be valid and acceptable by most authorities.

CHAPTER 14

SEXOLOGY

Dangers and pitfalls

The clinical study of sexual function is a legitimate area for physicians and psychologists, but the dangers for both patients and practitioners are only too obvious. The common problems in the male are: premature ejaculation (ejaculatio praecox), impotence, and failure of ejaculation; in the female: painful intercourse (dyspareunia), lack of libido, and failure to achieve orgasm (anorgasmia).

Discussion should be in the third person, not in the first or second; and the practitioner may never have recourse to activities which are morally objectionable in themselves. For example, it is very common for the sexologist with no clear moral principles to recommend masturbation as a "training" procedure. This is wrong and almost certainly harmful in the long run.

Another practice is to use surrogates as part of the therapeutic team, that is, someone who will stand in for the husband or wife of the inadequate partner and show him/her a few tricks. This is a pale passionless version of old-fashioned adultery and the surrogate is a thinly disguised prostitute on a salary rather than the more usual fee-for-service basis. The practice is obviously unethical and immoral.

The worst risk is that the doctor might get emotionally

involved with the patient, possibly as a matter of convenience (he is on the spot) or economy (no staff to pay), or perhaps he is unable to resist the sexual stimulus of the work. The hazard was clearly seen by Hippocrates 24 centuries ago, and was expressed in his famous Oath: "Into whatever houses I enter I will go into them for the benefit of the sick, and will abstain from every voluntary act of mischief and corruption, and further from the seduction of females or males, bond or free."

What protection is there for doctor or patient in this essential but hazardous work? Hippocrates had the answer: "With purity and holiness I will pass my life and practice my art." The modern Judeo-Christian physician will guard against evil by avoiding any compromising situation which might prove to be a near occasion of sin, strengthening his will by daily prayer and penance, and by seeing each patient as a suffering child of God.

Regrettably, the standards of the profession in this respect have never been worse. The first public revelation of the extent of this ethical malaise was at the Chicago meeting of the American Medical Association in 1973, where a survey showed that some 7 percent of doctors admitted to having had intercourse with patients. In the public discussion that followed, some of the ladies complained that, having seduced them in the modern fashion, doctors then went on to charge them the usual consultation fee! Should not the cash flow have been in the reverse direction?

Sex education

In the frenetic and confused world of modern pedagogy, doctors and nurses are often called on to give lectures on sexual matters. Judging from our performance in this area and the frequency of our marriage breakdowns, we should be the last to be offering advice. Only those whose personal lives are exemplary, loving and pure should be given access to the youth, but usually the reverse is the case. Sex education in public schools usually turns out to be instruction in contraception and subversion of parental authority. All forms of sexual activity are described to the children, the unspoken message being that since this is what everybody does and, since moral values are excluded, everything is permissible. The young are therefore introduced to masturbation, fornication and homosexuality at an early age. To mislead them like this is gravely sinful. "Woe to those who give scandal to one of these little ones," Jesus said (Matthew 18:6). This type of sex education has been described as "the massacre of innocence." Have people forgotten what Christ said about having a millstone placed about the neck and being cast into the depths of the sea?

In this regard, I have written a pamphlet on chastity for the young.[1] It offers 10 suggestions for youth to help them to lead decent lives and to keep their sexual experiences for marriage.

Pornography

There is no such thing as "nice," meaning refined, pornography. It is always vulgar and degrading, especially to women, and there are two features which are always associated with it: blasphemy and violence.

Whatever is evil hates what is good and innocent, and the ones who fill this description are: (1) Christ and the Blessed Virgin Mary, and (2) little children. Dante, in his *Divine Comedy* reserved a special place in hell for such as these. The violence which is induced by pornography is precipitated by the impure acts which it encourages. The incidence of rape and other violent sexual assaults has risen in parallel with the dissemination of pornography. This is the price society must pay for the sexual revolution. Sigmund Freud once observed that sexual abnormality is always associated with sadism and masochism. St. Thomas Aquinas (d. 1274) stated simply: "Impurity leads inevitably to violence."

The modern explosion of this type of printed matter, films, live shows, etc. is an unprecedented sociological phenomenon. Pornography is difficult to define but it is immediately recognizable. What has this to do with medicine? Simply that many doctors don't hesitate to prescribe pornography for certain of their patients. For example, if a doctor asks for a specimen of semen for fertility investigation, the laboratory will not uncommonly provide pornographic magazines to provide the stimulus. And sexologists or psychiatrists often suggest to patients that their sexual problems might be ameliorated by exposure to pornographic stimuli. It is a management that is almost certain to fail, and it will probably produce a worse state than the original. Except for those who have a professional duty to know about it (police, censors, medico-legal staff), exploring pornography is a risk to purity and therefore a sin. All those who cooperate in this evil in any way are culpable to greater or lesser degrees in their own and the personal sins of others to say nothing of their share of responsibility for the inevitable decline of the civilization in which we all live.

CHAPTER 15

MISCELLANEOUS MEDICAL MATTERS

Jehovah's Witnesses and blood transfusions

One must admire the courage and steadfastness with which Jehovah's Witnesses hold to their religious belief that blood transfusion is sinful and therefore never permissible. This belief is based on such biblical passages as Leviticus 17:13-14 and Acts 15:19-21, which forbid the consumption of blood.

The Catholic Church and most other churches do not apply this prohibition to modern blood transfusion. Even if the physician thinks that the basis for the Witnesses' belief is erroneous, his duty is to serve the patient and not to do anything that would offend that patient's conscience.

If the doctor is unhappy about this restriction on his management he should withdraw from the case, provided there is some competent replacement, but he may never force any treatment on anyone. This may mean that he has to stand by helplessly sometimes and watch a patient die from exsanguination, for example, in a case of postpartum hemorrhage, or a ruptured uterus, or an ectopic pregnancy or severe trauma. This is not suicide but a courageous, even if mistaken, decision by the patient. The doctor should notify the relevant medical and legal authorities to protect himself from subsequent charges of incompetence or negligence.

If he is presented with an unconscious patient, say, following a traffic accident, and there is no next of kin from whom to ask permission, he may assume the patient's assent and transfuse until consciousness returns.

A major problem arises when the patient is a minor and the decision not to transfuse lies with the parent or next of kin. A newborn baby, for example, might be suffering from Rh sensitization and profound anemia from blood destruction. An urgent exchange transfusion is needed to save its life. Since it is generally agreed that sometimes the state has the authority to step in, say, when parents are neglecting a child, or are incompetent, or criminal, or psychologically disturbed, it is reasonable to assume that, in these circumstances as well, parental authority is not unlimited, and a Court order may be obtained to do whatever is needed to save the child's life.

Genetics

This super-specialty demands not only complete knowledge of anatomy and physiology but also skill in mathematics and an ability to live one's whole professional life through a microscope. There has been a complete revelation of the mysteries of chromosomes, genes and inheritance in the last very few years. The International Genome project hopes to map over 40,000 genes and thereby extend our knowledge of life at the cellular level. It is the area in which many scientists expect to see the greatest breakthroughs in the area of medicine in the next decade or two.

The main ethical problems encountered in this specialty relate to genetic engineering and genetic counselling. In engineering, any intervention that aims at improving the welfare of the zygote or embryo is welcome, but if it seeks merely to manipulate the early human being for research purposes, for example, by cloning, this would be unacceptable.

Counselling is essential for parents who have hereditary or

familial diseases such as Huntington's chorea, cystic fibrosis, Down's Syndrome, NTDs and hundreds of other rare conditions. The common solution offered in these circumstances is usually contraception, sterilization or abortion, and as seen before, all of these are unacceptable. The only practical management is a system of natural family planning with intercourse limited to the postovulatory days. The counsellor advises the parents on the mathematical risk of future inheritance of their defective gene, expressed as 1:2, 1:10 or 1:100 chances, and they must then decide on their overall marriage policy.

Marriage rights

Have people with hereditary defects the right to marry and produce affected children if they so wish?

There is no doubt that the state has the power to prohibit marriage in certain circumstances. For example, it requires a certain minimal age for husbands and wives (usually 18 and 16). In the United States, it is common to require certain medical and blood tests before a marriage license can be issued. Long-term prisoners and psychiatric patients often lose their freedom to marry.

But it is a much more significant decision if the state moves to limit the basic freedoms of innocent and otherwise normal citizens. The best theological opinion is that couples do not lose their right to marry simply because of carrying defective genes. They must be credited with the capacity to live their lives in a responsible way and without paternalistic interference of the state. The modern history of the loss of human rights in so many dictatorships does not give one confidence in the decisions of states.

On the other hand, it is sad to see affected children being born from such marriages, a tragedy being worked out with an air of inevitability. Justice is being honored; but another one of the four cardinal virtues is prudence.

Case Report

Many years ago I had a patient who was blind. Like many blind people she was quietly proud of the way she could lead a fairly normal life, cooking, shopping, doing the housework. She then surprised me by marrying a blind man who, like her, could be described as just an ordinary person, not remarkable in any way. Their blindness in each case had an hereditary basis, and they were advised that any children had a 1:2 chance of being blind. Eventually they had four children, of whom two were sighted and two were blind. They all battled on bravely in life, but it was a pathetic sight to see the normal children leading around their afflicted parents and their two brothers.

They formed a happy family unit, they enjoyed life within their limitations, and they will come to the happiness of the Beatific Vision in Heaven. But was it prudent? Is prudence a greater virtue than fortitude? Is life a greater gift than the quality of that life and therefore worth more than a perfect existence here on earth? I shall never know the answer.

The physician and his colleagues

Ideally we should be a fraternity, a band of brothers (and, of course, sisters!), helping one another and all united in the one aim of serving the patient, whether directly in clinical work or indirectly in administration, teaching or research. The human condition is such that regrettably we are sometimes in conflict with one another. If we all adopted as our medical motto the phrase: *Caritas et justitia* (Love and justice) our problems would be much fewer.

Finances

Many doctors tend to be miserly, even though their financial status is usually secure. This probably stems from their long years as impecunious students or low paid hospital staff. In dealing with patients or colleagues, we should err on the side of generosity. Have you ever observed this extraordinary phenomenon, that, if we do make a foolishly indulgent donation or forego a big fee to an impoverished and sometimes ungrateful patient, even if we harbor an inner resentment, yet within a day our gift is often returned to us in some dramatic and unexpected way? It is, of course, the mysterious operation of a bountiful Providence.

Doctors deserve to earn a decent income because of the importance of their services, the long years of tertiary education, and the need to spend on equipment and postgraduate study. Fees to patients should be fair to all, keeping this in mind. It is, of course, unjust to "soak the rich to support the poor." Virtue lies somewhere in the middle.

Interfering in management of patients

To criticize a colleague to a patient or to alter his treatment is at least an offence against good manners if not against morality. But what should we do if we are certain that his management is either inadequate or dangerous? Ideally we should have the courage to discuss the matter with him in the first place — and be prepared to duck quickly. If he proves to be intransigent, the patient should be advised to seek a second opinion.

CHAPTER 16

NURSES, RESIDENTS AND STUDENTS

The role of nurses

One of the healthy developments in modern medicine is the recognition of nursing as a separate and independent profession, standing on its own feet. Nurses are no longer seen as servants of the doctors. Each profession serves the patient with dignity, with defined limits of responsibility but often with some overlapping. The specialties are independent but interdependent. Each could not manage without the other.

With the progress of tertiary education there are now nurse practitioners and university degrees in nursing. The nurse's first duty is not to the doctor but to the patient; therefore no authority, medical or otherwise, may order her to give or to withhold a certain treatment if she has a conscientious objection to that decision. For the doctor such an order would be *ultra vires*, a mistaken concept of his authority.

Having said this, there is no doubt that the doctor is the head of the therapeutic team and the nurse has an obligation to carry out his treatments, provided they are not illicit or harmful. It would be improper and impracticable if the nurse were to question his every decision, and if he had no confidence that his instructions for patient care were being carried out.

Fortunately, the two professions usually manage to live in a happy symbiosis, and advance together along parallel paths in an atmosphere of mutual respect.

On the other hand, with the popularity of militant feminism and the articulation of resentment of past oppression of the humble nursing profession, it is a fact of life that the more aggressive nurses now make life difficult for doctors, especially in obstetrics. An experienced midwife is a gem; she has acquired over the years an instinctive appreciation of the progress of normal labor, and she can diagnose early any danger to mother or baby. Yet she must put up with the frustration of working under inexperienced residents or students or young obstetricians. There is no way of ameliorating her nervous strain, apart from a saintly patience and a recognition that her services to the patients are beyond value.

The stresses experienced by the obstetrician must be recognized. Every delivery is an emergency and it is impossible, sometimes undesirable, for him to have to justify every decision or to explain every prediction running through his mind to either nurse or patient.

The ward nurse and the operating nurse each has special gifts, some practical, some more intellectual, and it is these that guide them to find their niche in the work he or she does best. Their work in the hospital makes them invaluable. If nurses recognized this it would increase their self-confidence, and they would not hesitate to take a stand against such unethical practices as contraception, sterilization, abortion and euthanasia. All good nurses, residents and students must have the individual and collective courage to refuse to cooperate.

Nurses as chaperones

Until recent years it has been the invariable practice to have a nurse present during gynecological or breast examinations, or indeed with almost any type of examination, but this seems to have gone by the board. Many patients have said to me that I was the first doctor they have ever consulted who had the nurse in attendance.

As a matter of good manners and refinement of taste, this service should be provided for all women patients. They should also have conditions of decent privacy for undressing and later dressing again.

The medico-legal societies constantly warn doctors that having a nurse present is essential for the protection of both doctor and patient. There are a few colleagues whose sexual standards are not above reproach; and sooner or later that charming little woman is going to turn out to be a paranoid and vicious obsessive who will accuse the doctor of indecent assault.

Residents and students

There is a clear urgent need for good young men and women to go into medicine and nursing, especially in the OB-GYN field, but the training calls for courage and persistence. This is not unexpected. If one wishes to follow Christ, the cross one takes up daily will entail a certain degree of professional and personal martyrdom.

Every city should have a Catholic (and a Christian) Nurses Guild, and a Catholic (and a Christian) Physicians Guild. These are essential for friendship, support and strength, but in practice the performance of the professionals and of the Church authorities in organizing such bodies is usually very disappointing.

A common feature of the training of future doctors and nurses is now to arrange visits to contraceptive and abortion clinics, ostensibly to enlarge the experience of the students in these areas.

The students would be well advised to decline the invitations politely and refuse to go. Anyone with perception can see that this is a thinly disguised example of the psychological technique of "desensitization." If they see what nice people work in the clinics and how sparkling clean they are, some may lose some of their abhorrence. As the Irish saying goes, "If you sup with the Devil, you need a long spoon." (Shakespeare has a similar phrase.)

CHAPTER 17

COOPERATION WITH HOSPITAL CHAPLAINS

The role of the chaplain

Despite the more enlightened modern attitude towards clergy services to the sick, there is still much room for improvement. The doctor or nurse with no religious experience often regards the hospital chaplain as irrelevant, even a nuisance. This myopic outlook stems from a century of secular education and the resulting decline in religious practice in the community. One encouraging fact is that the United States leads the English-speaking countries in regular churchgoing (some 20 percent of the population). In Britain the figure is only 3 percent! Let us hope that the Americans will lead the world back to sanity.

It is difficult for a proud profession to accept that the services of religion are more valuable than those of medicine. As a scientific discipline we deal with the physical world, but we fail to understand the metaphysical, which has more than three dimensions. Medicine concentrates on this world; religion on the next. If medicine limits itself to treating the physical body, we always lose the last battle in

141

life. But if we offer our patients love and justice, we always succeed. Science fails, but love triumphs. This is the apotheosis of the physician.

The chaplain, as a man of God, stands for love and justice. When there is nothing more that medicine can do, the priest is the only one who can offer patients a real service by bringing them consolation, acceptance, prayer, grace and the sacraments. The chaplain has a right to be at the patient's side, and we have a duty to facilitate this. We should welcome him as a professional colleague, and honor the value of his work. It is not only in terminal conditions that his contribution is of value. In any illness he helps the patient to appreciate the positive benefits of suffering, not just the character-building aspect of courage and endurance but also the penitential and redemptive implications of acceptance of pain. "Up on the cross with Christ...."

It is not only Christian, Jewish and Muslim patients who are receptive to the spiritual approach. I remember a pretty little Indian (Hindu) patient who was very worried about a bleeding problem during pregnancy.

"Are you praying to Shiva, Krishna and Vishnu?" I asked her.

"Oh, yes, Doctor," she said with wide dark eyes, shaking her head, "every night."

It was a touching statement of universal spirituality.

When ethical problems arise in medicine, the chaplain should be consulted before the doctors — he is the one trained in moral matters. The doctor is merely an amateur, this writer included. But in some countries it is rare to find a clergyman on a hospital's Ethical Committee. I wonder why?

Medical and nursing schools should have at least one lecture every year by a reliable cleric. He could ensure that all the staff know about baptism, its nature and how to administer it. The current ignorance about this simple but basic matter even in Catholic hospitals is unfortunate.

How much should the doctor or nurse tell the chaplain about

the patient's diagnosis? In general it would be prudent to limit oneself to generalities: the patient has a minor illness, or a chronic condition, or is *in extremis*. There is no need to provide him with the precise diagnosis unless there is a risk of infection.

Confidentiality (see also Chapter 4)

Preservation of privacy is the ideal, but it is always difficult for nurses and junior medical staff because they have contact with so many people moving in and out of the wards and clinics. Nevertheless, they should err on the side of saying too little rather than too much. In matters of health, illness and personal relationships the patient has a fundamental human right to privacy. At the same time, her family and friends always ask the important and impertinent question: What's wrong with her? The best policy is always to leave it to the patient to tell whomever she wishes, but if she is senile or comatose the next of kin should be the one to inform.

Never give confidential information over the telephone, even if the caller says he is the President or she is the Queen. To illustrate how cautious resident staff must be, the following episode occurred in one of my hospitals.

An agitated husband came to see the ward doctor one evening.

"Doctor," he said, "I've just got back — been away on business —and they told me my wife has had an emergency operation this afternoon. I'm worried sick. Is she all right? It's not cancer, is it? Oh God, I don't want to lose her."

"No, of course not. It's just a simple miscarriage."

His attitude changed immediately.

"Thanks, Doc. That's all I wanted to know. We've been separated for a year. I'm off to get a divorce. And you'll be called to give evidence."

Service to spirituality

Sickness is a time of great spiritual opportunity. When we are well and active we sometimes feel that we can afford to do without God, or at least postpone indefinitely our reconciliation with Him, but there is nothing like pain, or danger, or fear, or the prospect of death to remind us of our duties towards our Creator and the four Last Things (death, judgment, hell and heaven). As the Old Testament says, "Fear of the Lord is the beginning of wisdom" (Psalm 111:10).

CHAPTER 18

THE DOCTOR, SOCIETY AND THE STATE

The doctor and society

Since we are social beings as well as professionals, doctors exercise a profound influence on society. This influence is usually beneficent but sometimes unfavorable. Our first duty is to foster the physical and psychological health, not only of the individual but also of the social milieu. Only a few years ago, we were so inhibited by fears of being accused of "advertising" that few doctors would take a lead in the wider society. Fortunately those repressive days are gone and some even have the nerve to write a book (!), convinced that the pen is mightier than — if not the sword — at least the scalpel. We have a duty to speak out on matters affecting the well-being of patients or society. Not to do so might be a dereliction of duty, even if there is some risk of being misunderstood and attracting ill will.

The sexual revolution

The reader who has stayed with me this far will have some idea of the evils inflicted on society by contraception, abortion, sterilization, promiscuity, divorce, homosexuality and the other problems exacerbated by the sexual revolution. Much of this melancholy list could not have come to pass were it not for the cooperation, sometimes willing, sometimes under duress, of the medical profession. The main victims of this revolution are countless abandoned and abused women and children. There is evidence of widespread psychological and physical ill-health resulting from these practices, but the profession makes no meaningful protest. The Department of Health seems equally impotent. But they are very strong against smoking. Adolescent girls should be warned by the public health authorities that promiscuity carries the risk of STDs (including AIDS), chronic pelvic infection, sterility and cancer of the cervix. Young men should likewise be warned against sexually transmitted diseases and encouraged to take the lead in safeguarding the health, reputation and virtue of their girl friends. Both should be encouraged to live their lives in a responsible manner with the goal of becoming one day good fathers and mothers of families.

Alternative medicine

A burgeoning fringe of unorthodox (and sometimes dangerous) varieties of medicine bedazzle the patient in the modern world. They set one's head spinning. All too often patients end up going to quacks and wasting their money while risking their health and even their life in the bargain. What accounts for this therapeutic confusion? The first explanation is that medicine is not an exact science. The second is that the reparative power of nature, the *vis medicatrix naturae*, is so wonderful that most patients get better with passing time, even without the help of medication.

We have failed to convince our patients that orthodox medicine is the best, in fact the only, medicine — because orthodoxy, in science as in philosophy, is based on truth. Medicine tries to elucidate the scientific basis of the discipline, but to a certain extent it remains an empirical art founded on experience, prudence and common sense. The flourishing of unorthodox alternative medicine reveals a failure of general education. So many otherwise good people distrust orthodoxy and are unable to discriminate between what is true (hence good) and what is false (hence meretricious and dangerous) — in art or literature or politics as much as in science.

The question arises, "Who shall decide when doctors disagree?"[2] There can be no moral fault in giving patients what they want, providing that it does them no harm morally or physically — but it would be a serious fault to perpetrate a fraudulent, but fashionable, treatment mainly to make money out of gullible women. When it comes to allowing misleading, sometimes silly, medical theories to gain currency, surely there is some fault in this, even if it is minor. An example would be telling maternity patients that, if they will only practice some peculiar form of breathing, lie on the floor relaxing, and have their husbands massage various regions of their body, then they will be guaranteed a quick and easy delivery. Obstetricians know that they cannot predict from one day to the next how any labor will go.

Coping with the state

In modern times the power of the state, for good or for ill, has greatly increased and should be reduced. But the state controls vast amounts of money, and the harsh principle still applies: "He who pays the piper calls the tune." The aim of the medical profession should be, in the interests of both doctors and patients, to keep itself as independent of state financing and control as it possibly can.

It is proper for the state to ensure that the health of the individual and of the nation is preserved, which it does through the public health system, some hospitals, and coordination of educational and clinical services. It should facilitate the day to day work of family doctors and specialists in caring for patients. Regrettably, these front-line workers often form the impression that they are laboring in opposition to, rather than in cooperation with, the public health authorities. These latter tend to espouse left-wing philosophies, as do teachers and journalists, and they almost invariably support the various facets of the sexual revolution, including sex education in the schools. This presents a major ethical problem for physicians in government employment.

State torture

Fortunately in the West the state does not often require doctors to work against the interests of their patients, but even now in some countries they are occasionally involved in torture, psychological manipulation, use of "truth drugs" or even homicide. Under the Nazi regime, the examples are many of how doctors were engaged in experimenting on concentration camp prisoners, with most such experiments ending in death.

Dissidents in the former Soviet Union were often "diagnosed" as psychiatric patients and locked up in mental hospitals for the convenience of the state. One such victim, Anatoly Koryagin, was himself a doctor. Nominated for the 1986 Nobel Peace Prize, Koryagin, a psychiatrist, wrote a paper on "Unwilling Patients" in which he revealed how the KGB forced fearful colleagues to imprison patients and at the same time to degrade their profession. This courageous physician was in prison for six years and his health was permanently ruined by the ordeal.

It is hardly necessary to state that all these gross injustices are ethically wrong. What can state doctors do in these circumstances? To lead lives of moral rectitude, they must refuse to cooperate. But that might mean death! In a totalitarian state, daily life is really an undeclared civil war; and in wartime, death is a constant threat for all of us.

How could one possibly practice medicine in modern China with its harsh one-child per family policy? Stephen Mosher, formerly of Stanford University, has revealed how women pregnant for the second or third time are sometimes carried away and forcibly aborted even when well advanced in pregnancy. If the child is born alive, it is killed by an injection of formalin into the anterior fontanelle of the head. This must be the most inhumane and unjust legislation in the modern world.

In a similar but slightly less oppressive policy, Singapore in 1970 attempted to limit families to two children. It achieved this by financial and educational disincentives, which meant in effect forcing malnutrition and illiteracy on its own young citizens. The medical profession cooperated without demur. There never has been such a need for courage in this embattled fraternity.

But there is a glimmer of hope that common sense is emerging in national affairs in Singapore. The government has admitted its mistake, and 20 years later it is pleading with its women to have more babies. The demographic crisis, which could easily have been foreseen, means that the island-state is short of young men for the armed forces, and laborers have to be imported from Malaysia. There is no expression of remorse from the politicians and the doctors who brought the present situation about, however.

The change of plan will prove to be too late. For one thing, many of the citizens have been permanently sterilized; and for another, the populace which has been programmed to put the material welfare of themselves and the country ahead of every other consideration will not easily re-acquire an appreciation of childbearing. A similar drama is being played out in Japan and France.

Judicial execution

In recent years, some countries have introduced intravenous narcotics overdose as a technique of execution. Admittedly it is a more pleasant and tidier way to go than via the electric chair, or cyanide gas, or hanging, but the problem is to find a doctor or a nurse who is willing to set up the intravenous line and administer the drug.

Fortunately, the American Medical Association has had the courage to state that it would be unethical for a physician (or a nurse) to participate in such judicial killing. Their role is to save life, not to take it. If certain states legislate for this procedure, they should first work out who is going to perform the execution. Those states or doctors who support euthanasia legislation have placed themselves in a dilemma. If it is acceptable to kill the elderly and the incapacitated, why not criminals? It's a slippery slope.

The doctor's personal life

Is the private and personal life of the doctor of any concern to the patients or to anyone else? Must he live a virtuous and ethical life? Or may he be an alcoholic, drug addict, adulterer, practicing homosexual, wife-beater, liar or cheat? The answer is, naturally, that no one is free to indulge in these personal vices, least of all doctors and nurses and those in positions of trust in society. Patients have the right to be protected from such practitioners.

If a person has a serious moral flaw in his character in one facet of life, it will eventually affect his whole life. Medicine depends not only on love, but also on justice and truth. Science depends on truth. The researcher must be absolutely honest and reliable, even if clinical results disprove his precious thesis. To quote Hippocrates again, the ideal is: "In purity and holiness I shall pass my life...."

For those enlightened by the Judeo-Christian tradition, the basic rule of life should be morning and night prayers, a frequent lifting of the mind and heart to God during the day, and attendance at church or synagogue on a weekly basis. Even though a few may not measure up to this norm, the impressive fact is that the vast majority of doctors and nurses are good husbands, wives and parents, and they treat their patients with respect, devotion and tenderness. Their daily contact with suffering humanity and with death has a refining influence. The natural virtues (truth, courage, patience, etc.) keep them going and ensure an exemplary level of service to their patients.

Relationships with drug firms, medical suppliers, etc.

These contacts are necessary and fruitful; they in themselves have no moral implications, but it would be imprudent to risk professional independence through them. Drug firms and others perform an essential service, but they should not use doctors for advertising purposes. It is undignified, even humiliating, to be the recipients of pens, pads, diaries, free wines, free lunches ("there is no such thing"), convention sponsorships, scholarships, etc. If a drug firm pays the expenses of a physician to go to New York to give a paper on their new drug, doubts abut his veracity must immediately arise. He has compromised his independence.

I remember the embarrassment of receiving a large wall calendar from a good friend whose wife was also a patient of mine. Each page advertised: "Smith's Funerals Ltd." It gave the impression that we were somehow in cahoots; that I was putting a bit of business his way; and the patients probably thought that, if they did succumb as a result of my treatment, I would be getting a cut out of the funeral! Needless to say, the calendar ended in the wastepaper basket.

In my view, the Medical Association would do well to declare the receiving of gifts and favors as "unethical." The drug firms themselves would probably welcome such a move, as it would free them from the competitive expense and trouble of making these demeaning "hand-outs."

I was gratified to find that my long-standing prejudice in this matter has been shared by several writers in recent years. For example, Dr. R. Smith[1] stated that the Royal College of Physicians (London) had set out some guidelines to cover this relationship. In 1983 the pharmaceutical industry spent £5,000 per general practitioner on promotion of its drugs. Doctors had been given free travel on the Orient Express to Venice to hear about a new non-steroidal anti-inflammatory drug. Others had been taken on cruises to the Mediterranean islands. "The Committee regrets that refreshment at meetings are so often sponsored by pharmaceutical companies... It degrades the profession."

The physician's prayer life

The doctor without an active prayer life is an incomplete human being. There is nothing more pathetic than the person who has a brilliant intellect and knows something about everything in science, but knows little about history, literature, philosophy and religion. A large sector of human experience is *terra incognita* (uncharted territory) for him. Prayer is an important part of that broadening of the doctor's experience. Without it, his decisions ultimately risk being erroneous, even dangerous for individuals and society.

This concept was expressed elegantly and perceptively by Alfred Lord Tennyson (d. 1892):

> More things are wrought by prayer
> Than this world dreams of...
> For what are men better than sheep or goats
> If, knowing God, they lift not hands of prayer
> Both for themselves and those who call them friend.

Every day's work, every operation, should be preceded by silent prayer for the patients. And for the nurses. This is not a request for miraculous feats of diagnosis or for some scintillating operative *tour de force*. It is merely a dedication of our work and an acknowledgment of the fact, so easily forgotten, that we depend completely on God for everything. It is He who has given us the health and strength to do our daily work, the eyes to see with, the brain to perceive with, the grace to keep us ethically correct, the heart to love with, the courage to face up to sickness and death.

When we come to the end of our lives and face our final ethical assessment, God will not ask us for an account of our professional lives, our mortality figures, or the report of the Peer Review Committee. No, He will simply ask whether we have done our best, done the decent thing, upheld His standards of purity, justice and love. Did we have the courage to persevere in our moral standards in the face of the often intolerable pressures which are such a sad feature of so much of current professional life?

Shakespeare spoke to this recurring question in human life when he wrote the famous farewell speech of Polonius to his son Laertes:

> This above all: to thine own self be true,
> And it must follow, as the night the day,
> Thou canst not then be false to any man.
> (*Hamlet*, I, iii, 78-80)

In Christ's own life, His exercise of the human virtues of courage and endurance is often overlooked. He was surrounded by apostles and disciples who were weak, timid and treacherous men when He came to die. His Mother and the holy women at the foot of the cross showed up much better than did the men. Women almost always do! And they will save society from the evils that now threaten us all. But men will have to play their part, too.

These thoughts are expressed with greater clarity by the oft-quoted sentence of Edmund Burke (d. 1797): "The only thing necessary for the triumph of evil is for good men to do nothing."

Fighting against the evil of abortion and in favor of the right to life is one good place to start.

Saintly doctors

The patron saint of doctors has always been St. Luke, whom St. Paul described as "my beloved Luke, the physician" (Colossians 4:14). Luke went on to become the evangelist, the faithful biographer of the Divine Physician. The other historical patrons are Saints

Cosmas and Damian. Nothing definite is now known about their lives, but their cult was well-established by the 5th century. Tradition has it that they took no money for their services (which we all do on rare occasions), and once they miraculously restored a severed leg (which we never do on any occasion).

Since those ancient times, canonized doctors have been few and far between. Early in the 20th century Dr. Joseph Mosconi, a general practitioner in Northern Italy, was beatified. More recently Blessed Niels Stensen was beatified by Pope John Paul II in 1988. Stensen (1638-86) is known to all doctors by his original description of Stensen's duct, which conveys saliva from the parotid gland to the inside of the cheek. He was brilliant not only in anatomy but also in geology, chemistry and crystallography. He converted from Lutheranism, the State religion in Denmark, and became a Catholic. At the height of his fame he abandoned medicine, became a priest and later a bishop. These great men are ideals to imitate and to be the mediators for our prayers.

Physicians who swim against the sociological tide and refuse to go along with modern trends provide invaluable controls in what could well be a clinical trial of patient management. Many doctors, nurses and patients believe that it is impossible to live or to practice medicine in the brave new world without access to contraception, sterilization and abortion.

Judeo-Christian doctors can point to their thousands of patients and boast that these have not suffered from their ministrations. Their mortality and morbidity figures are no worse than those of their more "liberal" colleagues. In fact the opposite is almost always true. To trust the Church, to be convinced of the essential veracity of her guidance in ethical matters is the modern test of faith. There is no doubt that the Church has safeguarding the truth about the human person and the real long-term good of the patient as its goal. In this she is always right, and modern medicine often wrong.

NOTES

Chapter 2

[1] *Summa Theologica*, II-I, Q.19, A.5, 6.

[2] Further evidence that almost all of the great religions share the "Golden Rule" of justice and love in common is provided by the following quotes:

Christianity: "Therefore, whatever you want others to do for you, do so for them as well; for this is the Law and the Prophets" (Matthew 7:12).

Judaism: "What is hateful to you, do not to your fellow man. That is the entire Law; all the rest is commentary" (*Talmud*, Shabbat 3id).

Islam: "No one of you is a believer until he desires for his brother that which he desires for himself" (*Sunnah*).

Buddhism: "Hurt not others in ways that you yourself would find hurtful" (*Udana-Varga* 5, 18).

Confucianism: "Is there one maxim which ought to be acted upon throughout one's life? Surely it is the maxim of loving-kindness: do not unto others what you would not have them do unto you" (*Analects* 15, 23).

Taoism: "Regard your neighbor's gain as your own gain, and your neighbor's loss as your own loss" (*Tai Shang Kan Ying P'ien*).

Zoroastrianism: "That nature alone is good which refrains from doing unto another whatsoever is not good for itself" (*Dadisten-i-dinik* 94, 5).

[3] Pope John Paul II has decided to raise to the honors of the altar an Italian woman who died in 1962 when he beatifies Gianna Beretta Molla whose life was put at risk when she was carrying her fourth child. It was near the end of the second month of her pregnancy when a tumor was discovered in her uterus. Catholic teaching allows for the uterus to be removed even though that results in the death of the child, since the death of the child is not the intention of the operation. Mrs. Molla, a pediatrician by training, knew this but was adamant that the child live, even if it meant putting her own life at grave risk. Rather than abort the child, she carried it to term. A few days before the birth of a healthy girl with bright eyes whom they named Gianna Emanuela, she told her doctor and her husband, "If you have to choose between me and the child, don't worry. I demand you choose the child." The process for the beatification of Gianna Beretta Molla began in the Archdiocese of Milan in 1973 and is expected to conclude with her beatification sometime soon. (Cf. "A Mother With a Message," by Greg Burke, *Columbia*, April 1993.)

Chapter 4

[1] Faden, R.R. "Enforcing Informed Consent Requirements: Form or Substance," *Journal of the American Medical Assn.*, 1989; 261: 1948-9.

[2] Woods, W.D. "Informed Consent and the Need for Delegalization," *American Journal Disabled Children*, 1989; 143: 885-6.

[3] Silverman, W.A. "The myth of informed consent: in daily practice and in clinical trials," *Journal of Medical Ethics*, 1989; 15: 6-11.

[4] Dunn, H.P. "Unconsummated Marriage," *New Zealand Medical Journal*, 1958; 57: 156.

[5] *The Economist*, Jan. 9, 1993.

[6] Meyer, J.F., Reter, D. "Sex Reassignment — Follow-up," *Archives of General Psychiatry*, 1979; 36: 15.

[7] *The New York Times*, Jan. 16, 1983.

[8] Dunn, H.P. *The Doctor and Christian Marriage*. Alba House, New York, 1992.

Chapter 5

[1] "Nutrition and Hydration: Moral Considerations," *Linacre Quarterly*, 1992; 59: 8-30.

[2] Barnard, C. *Good Life, Good Death. A Doctor's Case for Euthanasia and Suicide.* Prentice-Hall, New Jersey, 1980.

[3] Smith, W.B. "Judeo-Christian Teaching on Euthanasia: Definitions, Distinctions and Decisions," *Linacre Quarterly*, 1987; 54: 27-42.

Chapter 6

[1] De Marco, D. "Ethical aspects of sex selection," *International Review Natural Family Planning*, 1985; Spring, 28-43.

Chapter 7

[1] Pride, M. *The Way Home. Beyond Feminism, Back to Reality.* Crossway Books, Westchester, Illinois, 1985.

[2] Gilder, G. *Men and Marriage.* Pelican, New Orleans, 1986.

[3] Cf. Llewellyn-Jones, D. *Everywoman.* Faber, London, 1980.

Chapter 8

[1] Dunn, H.P. *The Doctor and Christian Marriage.* Alba House, New York, 1992.
[2] Dunn, H.P. "The Safe Period," *Lancet*, 1956; 2: 441-2.
[3] Lloyd, G.E.R., ed., *Hippocratic Writings.* Pelican Classics, London, 1978.
[4] Provan, C.D. *The Bible and Birth Control.* Zimmer Printing, Pennsylvania, 1989.

Chapter 9

[1] Giovannucci, E. *et al.,* "A prospective cohort study of vasectomy and prostate cancer," *JAMA*, 1993; 269: 873-7.
[2] Giovannucci, E. *et al.,* "A retrospective cohort study of vasectomy and prostate cancer," *JAMA*, 1993; 269: 878-82.

Chapter 10

[1] *L'Osservatore Romano*, Sept. 30, 1992.
[2] Berkowitz, R.L. *et al.* "Selective reduction of multifetal pregnancies in the first trimester," *New England Journal of Medicine*, 1988; 318: 1043-7.
[3] Dunn, H.P. "Therapeutic abortion in New Zealand," *New Zealand Medical Journal*, 1968; 68: 253-8.
[4] Dunn, H.P. *So You're Pregnant.* E.J. Dwyer, Sydney, 1986.

Chapter 11

[1] Aristotle. *Ethics.* Penguin Classics, London, 1987.
[2] O'Connor, T.W. "Human Immunodeficiency Virus and the Surgeon," *Royal Australasian College of Surgeons Bulletin*, 1991; July, 30-31.

Chapter 12

[1] Dunn, H.P. *The Lancet*, 1959; Nov. 28, 1974. Corresp.
[2] Davidsohn, I. and Walls, B.B. *Todd-Standford Clinical Diagnosis by Laboratory Methods.* W.B. Saunders Co., Philadelphia, 1962. Page 926G.
[3] Dunn, H.P. "Semen Examination," *Linacre Quarterly*, 1987; 54: 88-90.

Chapter 13

[1] Dunn, H.P. "Obstetrics and the Christian Doctor," *Journal of Christian Health Care*, March, 1989.

[2] MRC Vitamin Study Research Group. "Prevention of neural tube defects. Results of the MRC Vitamin Study," *Lancet*, 1991; 131-137.

Chapter 14

[1] Dunn, H.P. *Should We or Shouldn't We?* Human Life International, Washington, D.C., 1993.

Chapter 18

[1] Smith, R. "Doctors and the drug industry; too close for comfort," *British Medical Journal*, 1986; 293: 905-6.

[2] Pope, Alexander. *Moral Essays,* 1773.